Moodle 1.9 Multimedia

Create and share multimedia learning materials in your Moodle courses

João Pedro Soares Fernandes

PUBLISHING

BIRMINGHAM - MUMBAI

Moodle 1.9 Multimedia

First published: May 2009

Production Reference: 1150509

Published by Packt Publishing Ltd.
32 Lincoln Road
Olton
Birmingham, B27 6PA, UK.

ISBN 978-1-847195-90-6

www.packtpub.com

Cover Image by Parag Kadam (paragvkadam@gmail.com)

Credits

Author
João Pedro Soares Fernandes

Reviewers
David Horat

Ian Wild

Laia Subirats

Acquisition Editor
David Barnes

Development Editor
Siddharth Mangarole

Technical Editor
Rakesh Shejwal

Indexer
Rekha Nair

Production Editorial Manager
Abhijeet Deobhakta

Editorial Team Leader
Akshara Aware

Project Team Leader
Lata Basantani

Project Coordinator
Neelkanth Mehta

Proofreader
Dirk Manuel

Production Coordinator
Dolly Dasilva

Cover Work
Dolly Dasilva

About the author

João Fernandes is a science teacher from Portugal, who has been working with Moodle since 2004. He has been involved in several Moodle initiatives at school, university, and government levels, as a teacher, trainer, course and content developer, manager, consultant, designer, and researcher.

João is currently living in London, pursuing a PhD in Science Education at King's College London and working on several projects on ICT in education. His main interests include education, multimedia, the Web, participation, democracy, and human development.

In a single year, he can be seen in several corners of the earth, either working, visiting schools, hiking, or taking photos in mostly non-touristic venues. He also loves music, old cheap cars, cooking, and spending his time with nature.

I would like to thank my family, friends, colleagues, and students for their support through the sometimes-painful process of writing a book while you work, study, and try to have a life. Thanks for all of the ideas and comments, and thanks for the shared experiences that inspired many of the activities in this book.

And thanks to all of the free software and free content communities for making great tools and resources available to everyone, and not just to some elite people. Whatever we do, is not just an achievement of one, but of many. This one is ours.

About the reviewers

David Horat was raised in Gran Canaria, a Spanish island near the African coast. There, he completed his M.Sc. in Computer Engineering at the University of Las Palmas de G.C. Encouraged by his colleagues and friends, he decided to go abroad. He spent six months on an Erasmus scholarship in the German University FH Nord Akademie, where he developed an eLearning platform based on Moodle and other tools. He later worked on his Master thesis, which focuses on accessibility and usability in web applications, but specifically as applied to Moodle.

David is currently working as a Software Engineer in the European Organization for Nuclear Research (CERN) specializing in grid technologies. He has also worked at Ericsson as a specialist on communication protocols. Among other things, he has participated as a Moodle mentor in the Google Summer of Code program for two years, contributing to the community in accessibility and usability projects.

Ian Wild is the co-founder of Heavy Horse Ltd. (`http://heavy-horse.co.uk`), a company specializing in information and communication technology, especially in the context of education. He lives in rural Worcestershire with his wife Karen and three children, Matthew, Lian, and Ethan.

Ian's career has always focused primarily on communication and education. Fifteen years spent in private industry, designing communication systems software, eventually saw Ian specialize in the design and development of access and learning aids for blind, visually impaired, dyslexic, and dyscalculic computer users—whilst also working part-time as a math and science tutor.

Teaching only part-time meant not spending as much time with his students as he would have liked. This, coupled with his background in learning and communication technology, seeded his interest in virtual learning environments.

Ian is author of the popular book *Moodle Course Conversion: Beginner's Guide*, also published by Packt.

Laia Subirats completed his M.S. degree in Telecommunications Engineering from Pompeu Fabra University in M.Sc 2008. During the last two years of her degree, she worked in several companies such as the European Organization for Nuclear Research (CERN), Telefonica R&D, and the Catalonian Supercomputing Centre. Thanks to the Google Summer of Code she worked in preventing, detecting, and solving Moodle usability problems. Moreover, she was a speaker for the Gradebook module in MoodleMoot 2008. Currently, she is studying a Research Master at the Telematics in Technical University of Catalonia, also in Barcelona, granted by the "la Caixa" scholarship program. She is especially interested in encouraging female teenagers into technical degrees.

I would like to thank my parents, grandparents, and aunts for their unconditional support. And special thanks to David for being with me in difficult moments as well as in the happy ones, of which there have been many more.

Table of Contents

Preface	**1**
Chapter 1: Getting Ready for Multimedia in Moodle	**7**
Multimedia in Moodle	**8**
About the course	**10**
Course structure	10
Course content	12
Pre-requisites	13
Knowledge	13
Hardware	13
Software	15
Configuring Moodle for multimedia	**16**
Three simple things using Moodle and multimedia	**17**
Task 1 – Adding images to forums	17
Examples of uses of a forum with pictures	18
Task 2 – Adding sound to forums	18
Examples of uses of a forum with sound attachments	19
Task 3 – Adding videos to forums	20
Examples of uses of a forum with videos	21
Summary	**23**
Chapter 2: Picture This	**25**
Finding free pictures online	**25**
The basics of image formats	26
Flickr	27
Uploading photos to Flickr	29
License	31
Wikimedia Commons	31
Other picture sites	32
Moodle it!	**33**
Uploading images as attachments	33

Using Moodle's HTML editor	34
Capturing and enhancing pictures using GIMP	**38**
Tips for effective photo capturing	39
Composition	40
Lighting	40
Size	42
Enhancing pictures using GIMP	42
Cropping	44
Resizing	47
Saving	49
Rotating	51
Flipping and rotating	52
Correcting white balance and color	52
Correcting brightness and contrast	54
Creating digital photo collages	55
Adding layers	55
Eliminating photo areas	56
Adding text	58
Capturing screenshots	**60**
Capturing screenshots by using the Print Screen key	60
Capturing screenshots using Jing	62
Creating comic strips using Strip Generator	**63**
Adding elements	65
Publishing	66
Creating slideshows	**68**
Exporting PowerPoint slides as images to build Moodle lessons	68
Publishing presentations using Slideshare	71
Creating online photo slideshows	73
Summary	**76**
Chapter 3: Sound and Music	**77**
Finding free music and sounds online	**77**
The basics of audio formats	77
Internet Archive: Audio archive	79
Freesound	80
CCMixter	80
Imeem	82
Uploading audio to Imeem	83
Creating playlists in Imeem	85
Other music and sound sites	88
Moodle it!	**89**
Creating and delivering	**89**
Extracting audio from CDs using VLC	90
Ripping a CD track	92

Creating and editing audio using Audacity 95
Slicing a track 97
Capturing audio from a microphone (line in) 100
Remixing audio 102
Converting text to speech using Voki **104**
Giving voice to an avatar 105
Podcasting using Podomatic **107**
Summary **113**
Chapter 4: Video **115**
Finding free videos online **115**
The basics of video formats 116
Instructables 116
Sclipo 117
TrueTube 118
Academic earth 118
Downloading YouTube and TeacherTube videos 119
Creating videos quickly and cheaply **122**
Grabbing video selections from DVDs 122
Editing videos using Windows Movie Maker 125
Creating a project 128
Creating a collection 128
Importing multimedia (starting with video) 129
Splitting 129
Creating a story board 130
Inserting transitions and effects 130
Inserting a title at the beginning of the movie 132
Inserting an image at the end of the movie 132
Removing the original soundtrack and inserting a new one 133
Publishing the edited movie 134
Moodle it! **135**
Uploading video directly to Moodle 135
Uploading videos to TeacherTube (or YouTube) 135
Creating a photo story with Windows Photo Story **138**
Importing pictures 139
Adding titles to pictures 141
Adding narration and motion 142
Adding background music 144
Publishing the Photo Story 144
Creating a screencast with Jing **146**
Recording the screen with audio 146
Creating an online TV station using Mogulus **148**
Creating a stop motion movie with Animator DV Simple+ **155**
Summary **159**

Chapter 5: Web 2.0 and Other Multimedia Forms 161
Creating gadgets to represent data by using Google Docs (Spreadsheets) 162
Insert a Gadget 163
Publish 166
Discuss, Share, Collaborate 167
Creating floor plans using a floor planner 167
Create a room 170
Add a floor 170
Add elements 171
Save and publish 171
Creating mind maps using Mindomo 173
Add topics 174
Add multimedia elements 174
Save and publish 176
Creating interactive timelines using Dipity 176
Add a topic 177
Add an event 178
Share 180
Creating custom maps using Google Maps 180
Create a new map 182
Add a placemark 182
Add a line 185
Share 186
Creating an online presentation using Voicethread 187
Upload media 188
Comment 190
Share 191
Summary 192

Chapter 6: Multimedia and Assessments 193
Adding multimedia to multiple choice answers in Moodle quizzes and lessons 193
Adding multimedia to quizzes, lessons, and assignments 197
Creating exercises with Hot Potatoes 197
JCross - Crosswords 198
JMix - Jumble exercises 202
Publish 203
Moodle it! 204
Creating interactive exercises with JClic 205
Start a new project 207

Creating a puzzle activity   208
Creating a finding pairs activity   213
Sequencing activities   214
Publish   216
Moodle it!   216
Assessing multimedia using rubrics   **218**
Criteria   219
Summary   **220**

Chapter 7: Synchronous Communication and Interaction   **221**
Communicating in real-time using text, audio, and video   **221**
Chat and group chat   222
Transferring files   226
Voice and video chat   226
Creating an online real-time classroom   **228**
Setting up a meeting   228
Starting a meeting   233
Sharing the desktop   233
Using the whiteboard   233
Uploading a Microsoft Powerpoint presentation or Adobe PDF document 234
Managing communication and participation   235
Recording   235
Summary   **235**

Chapter 8: Common Multimedia Issues in Moodle   **237**
Copyright issues   **237**
Fair use   238
Public domain   239
Licensing your work under a Creative Commons license   240
Referencing sources   243
Plagiarism   243
Seeking further advice   243
Safety issues   **244**
Personal details   244
Cyber-bullying   244
Seeking further advice   245
Selecting Web 2.0 applications   **245**
Moodle modules and plug-ins of interest   **246**
Summary   **247**

Index   **249**

Creating a puzzle activity	208
Creating a finding pairs activity	212
Sequencing activities	214
Publish	216
Moodle.fr	216
Assessing multimedia using rubrics	218
Criteria	219
Summary	220

Chapter 7: Synchronous Communication and interaction — 221

Communicating in real-time using text, audio, and video	221
Chat and group chat	222
Transferring files	226
Voice and video chat	226
Holding an online real-time classroom	226
Managing communication and participation	235
Recording	235
Summary	237

Chapter 8: Learning Using Time-Shift Master

Developing your work under a Creative Commons	
Looking further ahead	240
	244
	244
	244
Seeking further	245
Building Web 2.0 applications	
Moodle modules and plug-ins of interest	246
Summary	247

Index — 249

Preface

This book provides you with everything you need to include pictures, sound, video, animations, and more in your Moodle courses. You'll develop Moodle courses that you are proud of, and that your students enjoy.

This book was written around the design of an online course called Music for an everyday life using Moodle, where teachers and students will be required to create, share, and discuss multimedia elements. Music was selected as a starting theme because besides being fun and horizontal to all cultures, it's a subject that can easily gather contributions from areas such as Science (for example, Waves and Sound), Geography (with instruments from around the world such as the Ukelele), Languages (music in itself is a language), History (from medieval music to jazz), or even Social Sciences (for example, the law around creative works). It was not made for musicians in particular, and one of its main challenges was to reach different educators from different subjects. Music was the way to get these perspectives working all together.

The tasks presented are easy to do and consume as little time as possible, for teachers and trainers with busy schedules. We will use multi-platform, free software, and Web 2.0 tools to achieve this, and it was kept in mind that using multimedia is not just about improving instructions, but also to improve the ways in which students can construct. So a lot of the examples in the book will be based on activities designed for students in which they will be required to create, discuss and assess each other's multimedia works.

What this book covers

Chapter 1 takes a look at the evolution of multimedia—its advantages and uses in teaching and learning, and how these can be used with Moodle. We will also see some of the requirements for using multimedia in Moodle, and configure it accordingly, and make three simple experiments in a forum with pictures, sound, and video, to see if everything is working as expected in integrating these in Moodle.

We will finally consider the basic knowledge, equipment, and software required to start creating this course, Music for an everyday life, which will gather contributions from History, Geography, Social Sciences, Science, and other fields of human knowledge.

In *Chapter 2*, we will start by seeing how to find free pictures online to add to our course materials (and assignments, from a students' perspective) in services such as Flickr and Wikimedia Commons.

We will then have a look at different ways of inserting images in Moodle, especially using the HTML editor image upload function. We then start using GIMP for main image editing tasks, such as cropping, resizing, capturing (together with some photography concepts), color correction, photo collage, and saving in different formats. Some issues regarding images in Moodle, such as file formats and appropriate sizes, will also be discussed, and how to use the Print screen function and Jing to collect screenshots. Strip generator will be used to easily create comic strips. We will also learn how to export PowerPoint presentations to images, adding them to a Moodle lesson, or as an alternative publishing these presentations in Slideshare. We will conclude this chapter by looking at ways to create photo slideshows using Slide.

In *Chapter 3* we will focus on tasks for the Moodle integration of sound and music elements. The resources created will make information available in improved ways to students and will also get them to create audio artifacts, such as slices, remixes, voice recordings, text-to-speech, and podcasts.

We will use several tools to achieve this, especially Audacity, VLC media player, Voki, Podomatic, and Imeem and we will also see where to find free sounds and music on the Web.

In *Chapter 4* we will focus on video production and editing, looking at different ways of using these in Moodle. We will start by looking at places to find free video online, followed by ways of downloading videos from YouTube and TeacherTube, concluding with the basics of video formats. We will then look at ways of extracting DVD selections for later editing, and how to create photo stories, screencasts, an online TV station, and a stop motion video.

Chapter 5 focuses on activities that we can do with Moodle and some Web 2.0 tools. The objective is to show how this integration can open several possibilities for teaching and learning, providing free applications where teachers and students can create their own multimedia works and then embed them in Moodle for instruction, discussion, or assessment. We will create interactive floor plans, timelines, maps, online presentations, gadgets to represent data and mind maps. We will also see the possibilities of having collaboration in the construction of these multimedia works, as most Web 2.0 tools have as a standard the option to create with others a collective work.

In *Chapter 6*, we will learn to integrate multimedia elements in quizzes, lessons, and assignments. We will also use applications that allow us to create interactive exercises and games that can be easily assessed from and integrated into Moodle, such as crosswords, puzzles, matching pairs among others. We will look at rubrics as ways of assessing multimedia works in a quick and easy way.

Chapter 7 teaches us how to interact with students in Moodle courses in real-time by using an online chat service and a Web meeting tool. This will allow text, audio, and video chat and also whiteboard, presentation, and desktop sharing.

Chapter 8 deals with some common issues on multimedia in Moodle related to copyright, e-safety, referencing sources, and other similar issues. We will conclude with some possible modules and plug-ins to install in Moodle to expand its possibilities and some criteria for selecting Web 2.0 services for our classes.

Who this book is for

The book is primarily aimed at teachers and trainers who run professional courses and have experience in the use of Moodle. At the same time, it is not necessary to have an advanced technical background to create multimedia elements, as the tasks will be simple and as little time consuming as possible, relevant to everyday use.

Conventions

In this book, you will find a number of styles of text that distinguish between different kinds of information. Here are some examples of these styles, and an explanation of their meaning.

New terms and **important words** are shown in bold. Words that you see on the screen, in menus or dialog boxes for example, appear in our text like this: "In this case, we just need to provide the URL and click on the **Download** button".

Warnings or important notes appear in a box like this.

 Tips and tricks appear like this.

Reader feedback

Feedback from our readers is always welcome. Let us know what you think about this book—what you liked or may have disliked. Reader feedback is important for us to develop titles that you really get the most out of.

To send us general feedback, simply send an email to feedback@packtpub.com, and mention the book title in the subject of your message.

If there is a book that you need and would like to see us publish, please send us a note in the **SUGGEST A TITLE** form on www.packtpub.com or email suggest@packtpub.com.

If there is a topic that you have expertise in and you are interested in either writing or contributing to a book on, see our author guide on www.packtpub.com/authors.

Customer support

Now that you are the proud owner of a Packt book, we have a number of things to help you to get the most from your purchase.

Errata

Although we have taken every care to ensure the accuracy of the content of this book, mistakes do happen. If you find a mistake in one of our books—maybe a mistake in text or code—we would be grateful if you would report this to us. By doing so, you can save other readers from frustration, and help us to improve subsequent versions of this book. If you find any errata, please report them by visiting http://www.packtpub.com/support, selecting your book, clicking on the **let us know** link, and entering the details of your errata. Once your errata are verified, your submission will be accepted and the errata added to any list of existing errata. Any existing errata can be viewed by selecting your title from http://www.packtpub.com/support.

Piracy

Piracy of copyright material on the Internet is an ongoing problem across all media. At Packt, we take the protection of our copyright and licenses very seriously. If you come across any illegal copies of our works in any form on the Internet, please provide us with the location address or website name immediately so that we can pursue a remedy.

Please contact us at copyright@packtpub.com with a link to the suspected pirated material.

We appreciate your help in protecting our authors, and our ability to bring you valuable content.

Questions

You can contact us at questions@packtpub.com if you are having a problem with any aspect of the book, and we will do our best to address it.

1
Getting Ready for Multimedia in Moodle

Multimedia is a very old human endeavor. And curiously, it all started with images, more than 30,000 years ago, painted by pre-historic humans on cave walls.
The Chauvet caves and Lascaux caves, in France have the oldest paintings known to man (refer to the following image).

Source: Sacred destinations (2009).Lascaux cave painting. Retrieved April 14, 2009, from `http://www.sacred-destinations.com/france/lascaux-caves.htm` (Public domain)

This was the first technology invented to express and capture not only the world we experienced through our senses, but also our imagination and creativity in a medium that could be shared with others.

When compared to these paintings, written text is quite recent, and it marks the beginning of History, more than 9,000 years ago (that's the reason we call the period before it the pre-History). After stone, papyrus was used in ancient Egypt, then parchment, and later paper, invented in China and brought to Europe in the 12th Century.

The 19th Century saw great developments in multimedia. From photography to motion pictures, from mass production of paper to the new process of printing images and text on the same page, all of it was invented during this time.

Ironically, it took mankind almost all of the 30,000 years since the paintings on cave walls to get a combination of text, image, sound, and video, all working in the same medium. The first motion pictures articulating all of these elements were first watched in the 1920's, with soundtracks, subtitles, and of course, pictures — still or moving.

The real revolution started with the advent of computers and the Internet, and later on the World Wide Web in the beginning of the 90's, and economically-accessible technology for the masses. And finally, after thousands of years of human history, we (not just an elite few) can now create multimedia easily, and share it without great effort. In a way, it's a new era for human imagination, creativity, and expression.

This book is about exploring these new possibilities for not only we teachers and educators, but also we students and learners, for teaching, learning, and imagining in new ways, in our everyday life. And of course, we will be using Moodle for all of this.

By the end of this chapter we will:

- Know a little bit about the history of multimedia
- Understand some reasons for using multimedia in Moodle
- Attach a sound file to a Moodle forum post
- Embed an online video in a Moodle forum post
- Insert an image in a Moodle forum post
- Choose equipment and software with which to start creating multimedia

Multimedia in Moodle

Moodle was built around an idea of learning that happens when a group of people constructs things for one another, creating, collaboratively, a small culture of shared artifacts with shared meanings.

Moodle makes available many resources (web pages, books, files, links, and so on) and activities (forums, assignments, quizzes, lessons, databases, glossaries, and so on) to support teaching and learning, but what can distinguish working with these from paper and pencil work is the way we explore the possibilities of computers and the Web to articulate multimedia elements with text. Creating these multimedia elements, a very powerful concept too, is not possible using Moodle (it is not in its scope either), so when I am talking about using multimedia in Moodle I am mainly referring to the creation of multimedia using other kind of tools, particularly by students, and guided and later integrated, discussed, and assessed through Moodle.

Using multimedia in this way can provide more opportunities, to a group of teachers and students, for the construction of, in this case, **multimedia artifacts**. We will try to use multimedia not only as a product for better delivery, but also to improve the ways in which students can construct.

It is usually said that multimedia can be beneficial for learning, as it can approach diverse learning styles, add interactivity and learner control, and reduce the time required to learn or extend the information presented through different channels. When we talk about multimedia elements, we are talking about content; however, I would say that pedagogy is even more important. That is why we should also value diverse classroom practices around multimedia rather than just using it exclusively for delivery.

I would like to quote the words of Seymour Papert (1993):

> *Across the world children have entered a passionate and enduring love affair with the computer*

 Papert, Seymour: Preface to The Children's Machine: Rethinking School in the Age of the Computer. Retrieved 14 August, 2008, from `http://www.papert.org/articles/ChildrensMachine.html`

I believe that this also applies to multimedia — using multimedia in Moodle is a way of engaging our students and making subjects more interesting to them.

This book was written around the design of an online course called **Music for an everyday life** using Moodle, which is available at `http://www.musicforaneverydaylife.com`. This course is open to everyone (no enrolment key is needed; it has a guest access), so you can share it with colleagues as it is licensed under a **Creative Commons Attribution** license. This gives you a lot of freedom in using and remixing the course's content in your own course.

You might ask, why music? Music, besides being fun and horizontal to all cultures, is a subject that can easily gather contributions from areas such as Science (for example, Waves and Sound), Geography (with instruments from around the world, such as the Ukelele), Languages (music in itself is a language), World History (from medieval music to jazz), or even Social Sciences (the law around creative works). This book was not made for musicians in particular, and one of its main challenges was to reach different educators from different subjects. Music is simply the way to get all of these perspectives working together.

About the course

The main goal of the course is to develop a basic music literacy that can be used in the daily life of teenagers and adults.

I'm not a professional musician (barely a talented amateur) so I'm not expecting the course, Music for an everyday life, to be THE online reference in music education. Music was chosen as the main subject of the course so that it could be meaningful to as many people as possible. As it permeates all areas of life, I have tried to create a curriculum that reflected this, approaching music from a broader perspective, and not just basic music theory or instrument playing.

When designing this course, I tried to combine my experience in teaching (mainly science and ICT in education), and my time as a student in a Jazz school in Portugal, and all that teenage period that some of us go through, when we want to be stars, live somewhere between a studio and a stage, sell CDs, and be famous. Some of my friends who accompanied me during this period are now professional musicians (one has just graduated in the conservatory of Amsterdam), others changed paths despite their talent, and are now business men or designers. I became a science teacher; the studio times are gone, and I really like what I do now, but music will always be a part of my life, and this course was an opportunity to remember and share it with others.

Course structure

The course, Music for an everyday life, will be organized around 10 modules (adding one pre-session for preparation and one post-session for follow up), corresponding to three hours of work each, for a total of 30 hours. The course can be used either in distance education or combined with regular classes, what we call blended-learning or b-learning.

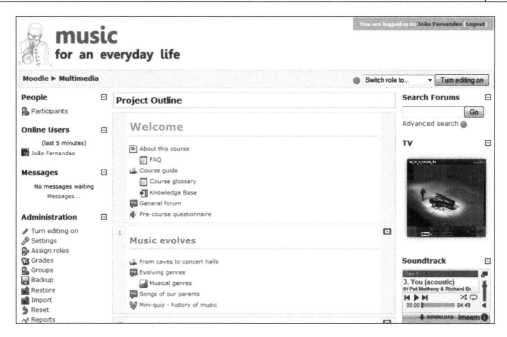

Each of the course's 10 modules will have a standard structure, starting with:

- One multimedia resource for a delivery moment
- Two student activities, involving the creation of multimedia artifacts (as a group or individually, computer based, online based, classroom based, or out-of-school based) with informal peer assessment and interaction
- One moment of formal assessment

For each module, we will develop multimedia content such as images, audio, video, and interactive content, so in total we will create some dozens of multimedia artifacts that are hopefully relevant, are easy-to-do, and are as little time consuming as possible to develop, for us teachers and trainers with busy schedules.

Course content

Using multimedia for delivery, and building our own teaching material, can be time-consuming, and as we know, being a teacher or a trainer is time consuming just by itself, without the need for any extra work load. This book will focus on simple multimedia elements that you can create without a huge effort, for your everyday life as a teacher or a trainer. Even if you are an enthusiast of digital technologies, keep this in mind—leave time and space for your students or trainees to explore the tools and create multimedia elements. Don't put all of the weight on your side. Better learning is not necessarily a consequence of instruction, so the focus of the course will be on giving the learner better opportunities to create and share multimedia artifacts, and to dialogue about and reflect on these constructions with others.

Nowadays, you can find a lot of free content on the Web that can be used for educational purposes without limitations. I would like to thank the authors of this content for their contribution to this culture of sharing in which we are now living. The same goes for the communities of free software, and the companies that provide software for free, for opening opportunities to many people, on which this book and the course are built upon. Building on their work is like "standing on the shoulders of giants".

The course modules will be organized around the following themes:

1. Music evolves—dealing with the history of music across the ages and within different genres.
2. A world of music—approaching the cultural diversity and music in different cultures.
3. Music and media—having a critical look at the message underlying music, especially in lyrics and music videos.
4. Music as a language—understanding basic music theory and learning to play an instrument.
5. Being a musician—exploring some daily events in the life of musicians.
6. Spaces for music—looking at music studios and technologies that support musical creation.
7. Music and the commons—understanding the business of music and alternative ways of licensing and distributing it.
8. The science of music—having a look at music from a science perspective, mainly sound and waves.
9. Music, dance, and emotion—exploring the links between music, dance, and emotions.
10. What's good music?—reflecting on quality criteria for music.

Pre-requisites

Some assumptions are made as the pre-requisites both for this book and for the course. These have to deal with the knowledge, hardware, and software that will be required to complete all of the proposed tasks.

Knowledge

The course will be for music beginners who probably have an instrument, such as a piano or guitar (this is not a necessity, as we will be also creating music using a computer), and who have an intermediate knowledge of how to use a computer, the Web, and Moodle from a student's perspective. This means that students are expected to already know how to manage files and folders, use a digital camera, and download photos and videos to a computer, how to install, uninstall, open, and close programs, and so on.

The pre-requisites for using this book are more-or-less the same, with the only difference being to know how to use Moodle from a teacher's perspective. This means that you should know how to create and configure resources and activities in general, upload files, use Moodle's HTML editor at least for text formatting, manage users, and run a simple course with forums, assignments, and basic quizzes (not, of course, for absolute novices in Moodle—there are some nice books from Packt if you need to improve your skills). If you are thinking that this is too much, and that technologies for multimedia creation are far too complicated for you or for your "older" students, have a look at this video `http://www.youtube.com/watch?v=pQHX-SjgQvQ` from the show "Øystein og jeg" on **Norwegian Broadcasting** (**NRK**) about a medieval helpdesk and this new technology called "book". I usually show it when the "age" argument comes up, and with it the usual assumption that older people can't learn a new technology. They can—it's just a matter of time and attitude.

Hardware

If you are on a tight budget, this is not a limitation for creating multimedia. It's easy to get a digital camera that, in addition to taking photos, also records videos, or to find a cheap headset that can be used to produce some sound, and all of this for less than €100/£90/USD$130.

A low-budget equipment kit

Digital cameras are now widespread and are an interesting replacement for a regular camera. They allow us to create pictures (and most of them allow the recording of videos as well) that can be archived to a computer, USB disk, or the Web. These days, even a regular mobile phone has a camera, so this can also be an option. You can also find cheap webcams and headsets. Thus, a low-budget equipment kit would consist of:

- A consumer digital camera that can capture videos
- A webcam
- A headset

A more advanced kit

If you want to spend a little bit more on equipment (and the budget allows this) you can build a simple home studio consisting of:

- An USB audio interface to which you can connect instruments and microphones
- A microphone with a tripod and a cable
- Headphones
- A mid-range webcam
- A mid-range digital camera that captures good quality videos
- A tripod for the camera
- A tablet
- A scanner

I will be using all of this equipment, plus a range of free software tools, to create the course, Music for an everyday life, always trying to select examples that can be transposed to other subjects. If you are an amateur musician, you probably know how to select this kind of equipment and will not have any problems. But if you are a science teacher, for example, don't worry. I'm a science teacher as well, just one who happens to have studied some Jazz, and the activities that we will perform will not demand any science or music knowledge. As I have told you before, the challenge of this book is to reach people in several subject areas. Let's establish a basic requirement associated with this book and with the participation, as a student, in the course in Moodle:

- A consumer digital camera that captures videos and photos with 2 Megapixels or more
- A webcam with a minimum of 640x480 pixels video and photo resolution

- An headset (better than just a microphone, because if you have the computer speakers on, there is the risk of feedback)
- A computer with an Internet connection (of course)

It is also assumed that the computer that will be used to perform the tasks of the course (and this book) has a Microsoft (XP or Vista), Macintosh, or Linux operating system and some minimum requirements, such as more than 512 MB of memory (ideally more than 1GB), at least one USB port, headphones, a microphone, the respective ports for these, and enough free disk space to install and use the applications suggested in this book (10 GB should be enough).

For the rest of the requirements, free software will do the trick.

Software

Throughout the course we will be using as much cross-platform, free, Open Source software as possible. However, in a few cases, the only Microsoft-compatible software will be the single choice (around four tasks will use Windows-only software) due to the lack of adequate alternatives on other OSes, or its broader distribution (this distribution will probably also apply to the readers of this book). Either way, as we will focus on processes and tasks that are "standard", I expect that these will also be useful, no matter which platform you use. Similar software for other platforms will be referred to as well.

Picking up software for multimedia production is very easy nowadays as many options are available for every need. Another challenge for this book is to select the ones with simpler interfaces, that are as multi-platform as possible, and of course, that are free. Sometimes, it will not be possible to get completely cross-platform software (software that can run in GNU/Linux, Mac OS, and Microsoft Windows), but such cases will be rare. The reason for selecting free software as far as possible is that it reduces the barriers to installation on schools' computers and students' personal computers (licenses for this kind of use are generally very open and usually free), so we can invest our money in equipment and time, instead.

As we go along building the course in the following chapters, other tools will be introduced. It's overwhelming if you get a list of 20+ applications to install at the beginning of the book, so we will introduce new tools as they are needed. Using many tools and strategies and lots of multimedia is not necessarily good, so the proposed tools will always have a context where they make sense, and can be used not only for improved delivery, but also for designing activities that are expected to motivate, engage, and create better opportunities for learning.

Configuring Moodle for multimedia

Moodle, as a Web based learning management system/virtual learning environment, is prepared for a range of multimedia elements (not for creation, but for integration). We can easily add images, videos, and sound files. And if everything works out as expected, we will just need to make a link to the multimedia file, and Moodle will do the rest to embed a player and show it.

However, there are some Moodle settings that we should be aware of that make this use of multimedia easier. We should ask our Moodle administrator to:

- **Enable the multimedia plugins**: In the Site administration block, go to **Modules | Filters** and click on the closed eye next to the plug-in name to open it). Then click on **Settings**, enable the **swf** plugin, and save the changes.

- **Allow the EMBED and OBJECT tags**: In the Site administration block, go to **Security | Site policies** and select the checkbox for this field, and save the changes.

- **Use the HTML editor**: In the Site administration block, go to **Appearance | HTML editor** and select the checkbox for this field and save the changes. This option is usually enabled by default.

- **Enable RSS Feeds**: In the Site administration block, go to **Server | RSS** and select the checkbox for this field and save the changes. After this, you will need to enable **RSS feeds** in each module that generates them: the **Database**, the **Forum**, and the **Glossary**. In the Site administration block, go to **Modules | Activities** and select the checkbox for **Enable RSS Feeds**, after clicking on the name of each of these modules, and then save the changes.

- **Increase the maximum upload file size**: Multimedia files can be sometimes larger than common document files, so having a good upload size limit will be helpful. A maximum upload size of 16 MB will be enough for common uses. If our Moodle installation has less than that, we could ask our administrator to increase it. In the `php.ini` file (or in the `.htaccess` file), change the following values: `post_max_size = 16777216` and `upload_max_filesize = 16777216`. In Apache `http.conf` or `php.conf`, change the value of `LimitRequestBody` to `16777216`. Then, in the Site administration block, go to **Security | Site** policies and in the dropdown box for the **Maximum uploaded file size** field, select the **Server limit**. Again, all of the Modules that allow attachments, for example, the **Assignment** and the **Forum**, will need individual configuration. Go to **Modules | Activities** and select **16 MB** from the dropdown box for the **Maximum attachment size** field in these two modules and save the changes. Also remember that teachers can change the maximum upload size for each course (go to **Settings**) and in each of these activities created in a course that allow file uploading.

Note that Moodle administrators can refuse to change some of these settings as they can overload the server, so we may need to ask them to upload larger files for us. Multimedia files, especially videos, can be very large files, so we should have some preoccupation with the size of the files we upload. An alternative that we will explore in this book is to host our files on online services and then embed (a concept we will see in a moment) these in Moodle. This will save server space for our school or institution, but can raise other questions such as blocked websites, bandwidth, or e-safety that we will see in this book. Another alternative is to use file formats that have good size/quality ratios, and we will learn how to select and use such file formats later on.

Three simple things using Moodle and multimedia

After going through these steps, it's a good time to try it out to see if everything is working. Let's start with three simple tasks, involving an image, a sound, and a video on a forum, respectively.

For further help and tutorials, go to
http://www.musicforaneverydaylife.com/getting-ready

Task 1 – Adding images to forums

1. Go to the Flickr **Creative Commons** (**CC**) licensed content at http://www.flickr.com/creativecommons/by-2.0 and search for a photo under an Attribution license (when an image is termed as CC attribution it means that we can use these images without any restrictions, except for needing to cite the author — we will have a look at copyright issues in Chapter 8).

2. On the results page, choose an image. Next, right-click on the image (if you are a Mac user and have a one-button mouse, click on it while pressing the *CTRL* key on the keyboard), and save the picture to your computer.

3. Finally, upload the image as an attachment to a new forum post, citing the source.

You should be able to see a screenshot similar to the following:

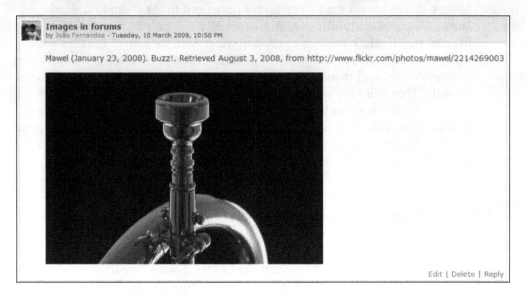

In this case, Moodle has automatically inserted the image for us. It has a width that will fit well in the screen. Sometimes, when the image has a width above say, 800 or 1024 pixels (depending on the monitor on which it is displayed), we will have to resize it, preferably before we upload it to Moodle. You don't have to worry about that for now.

Examples of uses of a forum with pictures

Pictures are sometimes better than a thousand words. We can use them in specific cases of the forum to:

- Share photos and report study visits
- Share and discuss a painting, a drawing, or a cartoon
- Create a collaborative photo story, where each post is an element of the story
- Share screen captures of works made with software

Task 2 – Adding sound to forums

1. Select a song from the Wired CD (`http://creativecommons.org/wired`).
2. Download it to your computer, again by right-clicking on the link to the music, and saving the target of the link to your computer.

3. Write a forum post in Moodle citing the source of the music (never forget the sources — the license of the music of this CD allows non-commercial sharing).

4. Upload the sound file as an attachment on the forum post.

 If you get an error in the upload, the problem may be related to the maximum upload size.

If everything works as expected you should see a screen similar to the following:

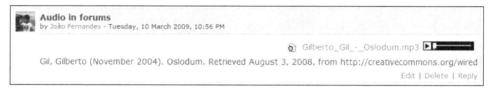

Moodle's multimedia plugin is automatically inserting a **Flash Player** for our MP3 file. The multimedia plugin processes the page, looking for links to multimedia files, and when it finds one, it tries to insert a player.

 In the case of MP3 files, we should ensure that we have the Flash Player plugin installed on our browser. We can go to http://www.adobe.com/shockwave/welcome and check this (if we don't have the Shockwave Player installed, that's not a problem). Flash Player allows the playing of multimedia content, such as audio, video, or animations inside browsers and nowadays it has become almost a standard on the Web.

We should also have the necessary players for file formats such as Quicktime Movie (*.mov files) and Windows Media Video (*.wmv files) installed on our computer and working inside our browser — for example, a Quicktime Player, available at http://www.apple.com/quicktime/download/.

Examples of uses of a forum with sound attachments

There are many uses for audio in other Moodle activities (such as the quiz or the assignment), but we'll just focus on the forum for now. We could:

- Share an interview or comment, and vote and comment on it
- Make a class selection of music themes
- Do a roleplay activity in which each student plays a character
- Ask for a poetry selection and declamation by students

- Start a collaborative and iterative composition of a musical theme, where each new post builds on the one before

- Generate a podcast through the conversion of the forum's RSS Feed

- Host a Q&A between the teacher, invited experts, and students

- Use a text-to-speech tool to create fictitious dialogues

- Do some ear training exercises

- Do a show-and-tell exercise

Task 3 – Adding videos to forums

1. Go to TeacherTube (`http://www.teachertube.com`) and search for a video. In the results page, choose one and click on it.

2. Copy the URL shown in the **Embeddable w/out Video Search** field that you will see to the right of the video.

3. Open a new forum post and write something about it. Do not forget to mention the source of the video.

4. In the HTML editor, use the *Enter* key after the source and then click on the **< >** button to switch to HTML mode. Paste the code after the HTML tag **
** (which corresponds to a line break in the text), as shown in the following screenshot:

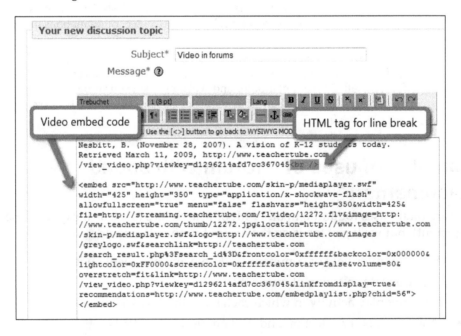

5. Post your message, and the result will look similar to the following screenshot:

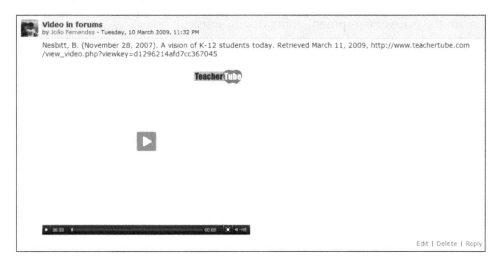

This embed procedure is very helpful, and you should keep these very simple steps in mind:

1. Copy the embed code.
2. Click on the **< >** button in the HTML editor.
3. Paste the embed code.

In a post, the size of the video (width and height) will fit well in the screen, but if we were embedding it in a Moodle block, we will have to change something in the code used "as is". We will leave that for later, when it's needed.

Examples of uses of a forum with videos

Using forums with videos is a great way to start a discussion, and it can also be used to:

- Comment on a video excerpt
- Create a collaborative video selection
- Broadcast a live event
- Post a video to add subtitles and comments
- Post a silent video for students to submit a soundtrack
- Post a video tutorial capturing procedures for a software application

We have just tried three simple examples of using content that was not made by us. Creating our own multimedia content is another story; but nowadays it can be quite easy, with the price of equipment going down, software interfaces getting simpler to use, and a wide variety of free software being available for multimedia editing. We now don't have any excuses for not using it, except for a lack of time. The subsequent chapters in this book will deal with this multimedia production, explaining and showing how to create these resources for delivery and active learning, not just as products, but also as activities for your students to participate in.

To give you just a flavor of what the course will be, here is a list of some examples that will be developed either for the course by the teachers, or during the course activities by the students:

- Add short audio clips and voice recordings to forums
- Produce video tutorials explaining some tasks in music software and exploring some web sites
- Add a soundtrack and remix a video
- Broadcast a live video through Moodle
- Create an interactive timeline of the history of music
- Create a collective world map with multimedia place marks of world instruments
- Design a music studio floor plan
- Draw a cartoon strip about a scene in the life of a musician
- Direct a stop-motion animation
- Create a collaborative multimedia music styles glossary
- Create interactive diagrams and charts
- Use multimedia Moodle quizzes, lessons, and assignments with multimedia
- And many other such exciting activities!

Summary

We have had an overview of the evolution of multimedia, considering some of the potential advantages of its uses in teaching and learning. These uses can be aligned with the underlying learning philosophy of Moodle, focusing not just on delivery but also on active learning, where students will use the tools for multimedia creation to augment their possibilities to construct, share, dialogue with, and reflect upon those constructions with others.

We also considered the basic knowledge, equipment, and software required to start creating our course, Music for an everyday life, which will gather contributions from History, Geography, Social Sciences, Science, and other fields of human knowledge. And finally, we saw some of the requirements for using multimedia in Moodle, and made three simple experiments on a forum, with pictures, sound, and video, to see if everything was working as expected.

So, let's start, just like the Chauvet and Lascaux caves, with images!

2
Picture This

This chapter will essentially focus on creating and editing pictures for the course Music for an everyday life, which includes finding free pictures online, making photo collages, and comic strips, or just simple screenshots and slideshows. We will also have a look at some basic photography concepts so that we can start creating and enhancing some nice photos for our course.

By the end of this chapter you will be able to:

- Use a set of free software tools for common procedures in picture editing
- Create and edit photos for the course
- Select appropriate image formats according to your needs
- Integrate images in Moodle

Finding free pictures online

Reinventing the wheel, especially for teachers, is a great path to burn-out. Creating pictures for our courses (photos, drawings, and icons), if we are working from scratch, is extremely time-consuming, adding to the course design effort, interaction with students, or worse, assessment. Fortunately, we are not working alone anymore, as there are many places on the Web where, with the help of millions, we can get ready-made pictures, for free (well, sometimes searching for a nice picture can take a while, but it can be worth the effort!). But first, let's take a look at the basic image formats, before we go on to see the places where we can find free online pictures.

The basics of image formats

There are some things that we should know about image formats, particularly how to choose the best formats for our Moodle courses. There are many formats around, but the good news is that we will just need to use four of these in our daily life:

- **GIF**: It's an old format that only uses 256 colors, so it can be useful for storing simple images with few colors, such as logos or diagrams. This format also supports animation (animated GIFs). Avoid it when storing more complex pictures such as photos of landscapes.

- **PNG**: It's an enhancement to the GIF format, supporting 16 million colors, and was created as an open source alternative to GIF. It's a good format for storing images that are being edited.

- **JPEG**: A very common format on the Web and for digital cameras. It has a good quality/file size balance, so if we need to save on space, this can be a good format to choose. It uses image compression. However, if we use this format when editing images (repeatedly, saving each that time we make any changes to it) we will lose image quality. So to avoid this, when editing, use other formats such as PNG. When you want to publish it on the Web or just send it by e-mail, then go for JPEG. The file extension is JPG.

- **BMP**: An image format from Microsoft (for example, Paint uses it), usually corresponds to huge file sizes, so the best thing to do is to convert it to one of the preceding formats, depending on the kind of image and what you want to do with it.

Sometimes it's not just about image formats. For example, we can have huge JPEG files captured in digital cameras with 12 Megapixels. In this case, scaling the image to smaller sizes (that will fit well in a screen, if we are talking about using them in Moodle) is the way to go. We will see how to scale images and convert them in any of these four image formats in this chapter.

Flickr

Flickr (`http://www.flickr.com`) is a great online service for organizing, publishing, and sharing photos (or screenshots) and for meeting people with the same interests. It has millions and millions of photos, including Creative Commons licensed photos, as we saw earlier. Among many other things, it allows you to organize photos in sets, edit them, create slideshows, and even overlay photos in an online map. In the Creative Commons section of Flickr (`http://flickr.com/creativecommons`), we can get millions of pictures licensed under Creative Commons licenses, meaning that we can use them in general for educational purposes without major limitations (especially with the Attribution only licenses). To learn more about these licenses, check the last chapter in this book or read the brief explanations in Flickr about them, shown on the right in the screenshot below. We will talk a lot about these licenses as we move ahead with the book.

To search for pictures we must first click on the **See more** link for the type of licensed photos that we want to use (there is a brief description of the available licenses on the right side of the screen, and also in Chapter 8 of this book) and then use the search form available at the top of the page, typing the keywords that we are looking for:

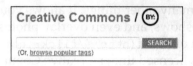

Once we are on the results page, we can click on one of the search results. We get a screenshot similar to the following:

Just to remind you of how to save a picture from the Web to our computer, here is the basic procedure:

1. Right-click on (or hold the *CTRL* key and click if you're a Mac user) the picture displayed in the web browser.

2. From the menu that appears, select the **Save image as...** option.

3. Select a destination on your computer and save the image to this location.

Source: Nzgabriel (2008, July 11). Trumpet. Retrieved August 10, 2008,
from `http://flickr.com/photos/nzgabriel/2659330391/`

Every time we save a picture, we must not forget to register some details about it, to properly reference it later in our Moodle course (author, date, page title, picture title, link). See Chapter 8 for more details on referencing sources.

Flickr pictures are displayed on the screen with a typical size for Web display (it's a way of keeping the images with sizes that are appropriate to several screen sizes and internet connections), but if you click on the magnifier **All sizes** link above the upper-left corner of the image, you can get pictures at smaller or larger sizes.

Because the Web is not just about taking but also about giving, next we will see how to upload our own photos to this service, so that others can build on our work too.

Uploading photos to Flickr

The approach we will mainly use in this chapter with regard to pictures in Moodle is to upload images to our course, either to the course's files area or as an attachment in several activities. However, if we want to participate in a broader community of sharing (not just in our small course), a solution would be to post the pictures on Flickr, where they will be available to many people, and will constitute a kind of repository of images that we can use in several Moodle courses. But it's not just about sharing or making management easy. It's also about getting feedback from others, contacting the "real" world, and engaging in conversations about our work. This is a huge opportunity (with risks, if we are talking about students posting their photos — see Chapter 8 for a discussion about these concerns on safety) for learning, and a way of participating in the community.

To make photo uploads easier, in addition to using the Web interface, we can download and install an official uploader, the **Flickr Uploadr** (go to `http://www.flickr.com/tools/`). We will use this upload tool to create our first photo set. After installing it, we will need to follow the steps shown below:

1. Click on the **Sign in** button, to sign in to Flickr. The first time that we connect to the service, we will have to authorize the connection, by going to Flickr and following the instructions provided.

2. Add photos to the left panel of the Flickr Uploadr, either by dragging photos from the file explorer or by clicking on the **+Add** button.

3. Click on the **CREATE A SET...** link in the panel on the right, fill in the forms, and start uploading. It's as simple as that!

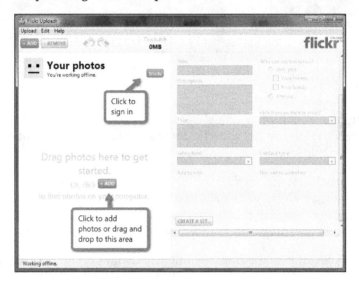

With a free account, we can create just three sets! Upgrading to pro will let us create as many sets as we want.

After we have the photos online we can insert them into our course by using the HTML editor — in this case adding the URL to the photo in Flickr instead of uploading the image to Moodle. However, the photo has to link back to the photo page as this is required by the terms of service of Flickr. We can do this easily by adding the link to that page below the picture, again using the HTML editor.

It's also worth mentioning Picasa (`http://picasa.google.com`), another service for publishing images online, that we can use to organize our photos.

License

In the account preferences, concerning the license of the photos that we put online on Flickr (`http://www.flickr.com/account/prefs/license`), we can associate them automatically (with the possibility of changing it at any time) to a Creative Commons license of our choice. This can also be done by using a batch edit. This batch editing (`http://www.flickr.com/photos/organize`) allows the control of permissions and even editing (for example, making some photos private, others all rights reserved, rotating, and so on).

Wikimedia Commons

Wikimedia Commons (`http://commons.wikimedia.org`) is a project by the Wikimedia foundation, the same one that is responsible for Wikipedia. Wikimedia Commons hosts all of the pictures and other multimedia elements (audio, video, and vectors) included in the well known Wikipedia online encyclopedia articles. We can find interesting pictures on a variety of topics (using the **search** form on the left-most side of the screen), mainly under **GNU Free Documentation** and Creative Commons licenses, so we can use these without many limitations in our courses.

Other picture sites

In addition to these two services, we can find many other online services where we can obtain pictures, such as:

- Stock Exchange (`http://www.sxc.hu`) - an online service where we can download as many pictures as we want, for free.

- Shutterstock (`http://www.shutterstock.com`) - a commercial service that makes available royalty-free drawings and photos. These kinds of services are usually available through a subscription service, in which we can download a limited number of photos for a fee.

In the course, I have used several pictures from these sources to create delivery moments, for example, in *Module 7 - Music and the commons*, I have used the following image:

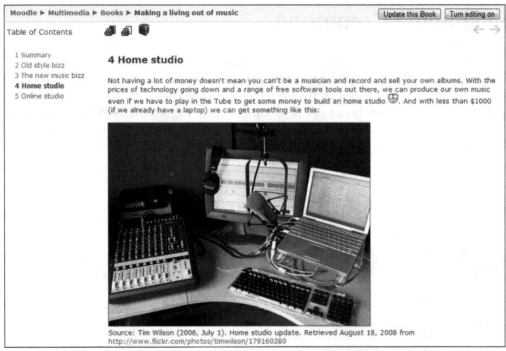

Source: Tim Wilson (2006, July 1). Home studio update. Retrieved August 18, 2008 from `http://www.flickr.com/photos/timwilson/179160280`

Moodle it!

Inserting images in Moodle is really easy. Now that we have a source of free pictures for our course, there are several ways to insert them, depending on the type of resource or activity that we are using. We will have a look at the following three ways in this book:

- Uploading images as attachments (for example, in forums, glossaries, or databases).

- Using the built-in HTML editor and the course files area to store the images.

- Embedding HTML code (specific for images) on web forms. (Don't be scared, it's easy and can be helpful on some occasions, just as we saw with YouTube videos. We will use it later in Chapter 5 for adding pictures to Google Maps, for example).

For now, let's just look at the first two ways of inserting images.

Uploading images as attachments

Using attachments is the easiest way to add a picture to Moodle. This possibility is available for some activities in Moodle, such as the forum, glossary, and database, and it's the easiest way for students to submit their pictures to a course, as they don't have write access to the course files area. We saw in Chapter 1 how we could do this in a forum. Basically, this is the same process of adding an attachment to an e-mail, but in this case Moodle does the rest to display the image on the forum post (it generates the HTML code needed for this). There is just one thing to keep in mind — when we add a picture as an attachment, it will be displayed in its original size. This means that if our image is too large for the screen size we are using, we will have a problem in visualizing it. In a moment we will see how to resize a picture to make it fit well for our course.

In the glossaries in the encyclopedia display format, images added as attachments are shown inline. In *Module 1 - Music evolves*, students are required to add a course glossary about an artist their parents like, with one photo and a music track. When adding an entry, we have a field to insert an attachment:

When we save the entry, we will have a glossary entry something like this:

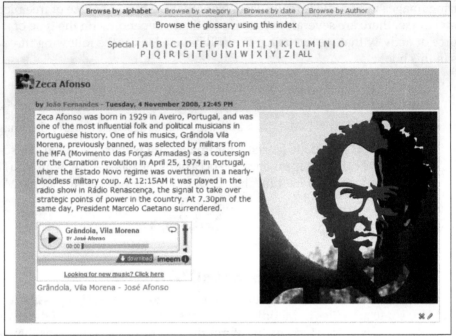

Source: Juntas (2006, May 1). File:José Afonso - Monumento em Grandola1.JPG. Retrieved February 2, 2009 from http://en.wikipedia.org/wiki/Image:Zeca_afonso2.jpg

The small player on the left in the glossary entry above is taken from Imeem, an online community about music, and we will see how we can use it in the next chapter, which is about sound and music.

Using Moodle's HTML editor

Using Moodle's built-in HTML editor and the course files area is a simple way of inserting images in Moodle, in side blocks or in any kind of resource or activity. The basic procedure for doing this is:

1. Send the image to the course's files area.
2. Insert the image in our content.
3. Save your changes.

When we create content in Moodle, by default we have access to a word processor-like toolbar that helps us format text in what is called a **WYSIWYG (What You See Is What You Get)** interface. In this kind of interface we can see how the content will look as we make the changes (refer to the following screenshot).

Many of the buttons of this toolbar are fairly standard, but there are some that are not so familiar. However, all software toolbars show hints about the buttons if we hover the mouse over the buttons. This will help us to know their functions and will be extremely useful during the course of this book. In the following screenshot, the little button representing a framed landscape in the toolbar's second row, shows its function when the mouse is over it (no need to click!), that is, **Insert Image**:

After we click on the button, the following window appears:

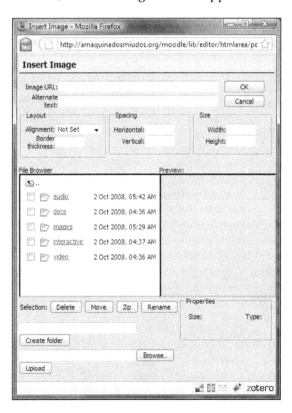

This is the standard window for uploading images to Moodle, and is slightly different to the interface for managing files in the administration block. In addition to creating folders and uploading and managing files, we can also preview the pictures, define their layout, or add alternative text (the text that is displayed when you hover the mouse over the picture).

In the **File browser** dialog box, we can see the folders that have already been created to organize the content in one of the course modules (**audio, docs,** and so on), in this case *Module 1 – Music evolves*. We will be adding a photo of a Neolithic flute found in China, taken from Wikimedia Commons, to our Moodle book "From caves to concert halls" in this module. For this:

1. Click on the destination folder in the course's files area (in this case the **images** folder where all of the modules' images will be stored).
2. Click on the **Browse...** button and select the picture from your computer.
3. Click on the **Upload** button.
4. The file will be uploaded to the course's files area, and if we click on the file name in the **File browser** area, two things will happen. Firstly, a preview of the picture will be shown in the **Preview** area on the right, and secondly, the **Image URL** form on the top will automatically be filled in.

We will get something similar to the following:

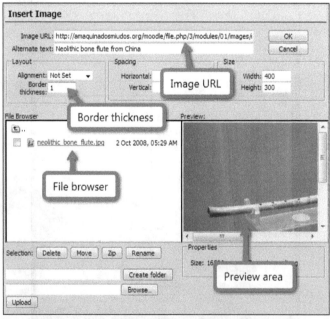

Source: asgitner (2007, January 7). File:Neolithic bone flute.jpg. Retrieved September 12, 2008 from http://en.wikipedia.org/wiki/File:Neolithic_bone_flute.jpg

Note the two things that can be useful, and that were changed in the preceding window:

- In the **Layout** area, we can insert a **border thickness** of **1**. This will add a black border that is one pixel wide around the picture.

- We must also add an **Alternate text** at the top of the window, in this case **Neolithic bone flute from China**. This is required as an accessibility standard, so that screen readers can "read" images (what they will read is this alternate text describing the image)

Now, something important. After we click on the **OK** button, we are taken back to the HTML editor view, and if we click on the image, we can resize it by dragging one of the corners of it while holding down the mouse button. I wouldn't recommend this, as the image will lose a lot of quality. The best thing to do is to resize the image in an image editing software application and then upload it to our course, as we will see in this chapter. You can see some reference values for image sizes in Moodle in this chapter, when we talk about resizing procedures.

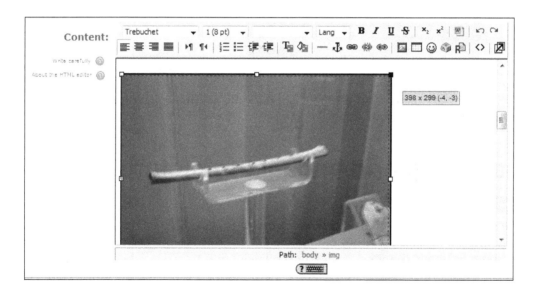

When we save our changes, the image will be inserted in the book and we will get a screenshot similar to the following:

The first instrument

It is possible that the first musical instrument was the human voice itself, which can make a vast array of sounds, from singing, humming and whistling through to clicking, coughing and yawning. The oldest known Neanderthal hyoid bone with the modern human form has been dated to be 60,000 years old, predating the oldest known bone flute by 10,000 years; but since both artifacts are unique the true chronology may date back much further! Most likely the first rhythm instruments or percussion instruments involved the clapping of hands, stones hit together, or other things that are useful to create rhythm and indeed there are examples of musical instruments which date back as far as the paleolithic (Wikipedia, 2008).

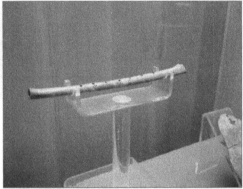

One of the gudi flutes discovered at Jiahu, China, on display at the Henan Museum

Now that we are ready to insert images in Moodle, let's have a look at how to capture and enhance pictures.

Capturing and enhancing pictures using GIMP

The usual cliché "a picture is worth more than a thousand words" sometimes convinces me. Especially, if we are talking about our students creating these images, by photographing, drawing, or making collages, and discussing these with their peers. Using strong images to introduce themes is a great starter and a nice context to question students. Pictures seem to resonate with many students in textbooks, course material, illustrating reports, raw material for photo stories or story boards, and as assignment products in general. Give students a digital camera and they'll just start photographing and filming without any limitations. And now it's quick and cheap to take even a thousand photos.

As teachers, we also use a lot of pictures in presentations, exams and exercises, department or club panels, to photograph experiments, activities and students' works, to create mascots made of collages, and many other things. I did all of this as a teacher, and I particularly enjoyed making those mascots—for example using the face of my school's patron with different bodies to publicize events (such as a vampire in a blood collection that was open to the community, a nurse for health week, or a mad scientist during a science week). All of these were huge successes in the school, and a great laugh too!

Let's leave the mascots aside and begin learning photo capturing.

Tips for effective photo capturing

One of the activities in our course consists of students putting together a budget for a music studio, which involves doing some research on equipment and prices, visiting real studios around their locality and taking some photos with a digital camera (a pre-requisite of the course) of the solutions adopted in these studios, creating a budget using an online spreadsheet, and finally submitting everything to the Moodle course.

Giving a digital camera to students without major guidelines, especially if they are going to take photos with interior lighting in music studios, will probably result in problems of file size, lighting and/or focus. However, lets not make it complicated—digital cameras these days can do fairly well without manual control. So let's just have a look at some basic tips for effective capturing.

There are three basic things that we should take into account when taking photos:

- Composition—how the "subject" (not necessarily a person) in a picture is framed
- Lighting—the sources of light and the related shadows
- Size—the number of pixels (the indivisible points) that a picture is made of

Composition

There is a basic rule of composition called the **Rule of thirds** that states that the main element we want to photograph should be at one of the intersection points of four imaginary lines that divide the picture into nine equal-shaped areas:

Source: eyeliam (2008, June 8). IMG_6304. Retrieved August 12, 2008 from
http://www.flickr.com/photos/eyeliam/2544346949/

Notice that the slider in the mixer above (the "subject") is in one of these intersection points. Many digital cameras have this option to show the Rule of thirds so that we can frame the picture easily by overlaying these lines in the camera's viewfinder. If not, it's just a matter of imagining the lines.

Lighting

Using a digital camera indoors can result in really bad photos. As interior lighting is usually more limited than outdoors, if we are using the camera in automatic mode this will probably require flash or the photos will be blurry (and particularly if we are not using a tripod). Flash can be a problem if you want to keep the colors and original lighting of the interiors, and also has the limitation of giving the foreground a big burst of light while the background is left completely dark. A typical range of flash light is around one to three meters, so taking photos of a studio will almost certainly have these results.

One alternative to the flash is to use the camera with a tripod in manual mode, and control the shutter speed and aperture.

- Shutter is the mechanical part that blocks all light from exposing the film (in the case of digital cameras, the CCD sensors) until you press the button. Then it quickly opens and closes, letting the light in the camera through the lens. You can control the amount of time that the shutter remains open by setting the **shutter speed** in your camera settings. The typical values range from 1/250th of a second to a couple of seconds.

- Aperture typically refers to the diaphragm aperture, which can be adjusted to vary the size of the pupil, and hence the amount of light that reaches the CCD sensor. Aperture is expressed in the form f/value, meaning that the smaller the value, the larger the lens opening (aperture). There is a so-called **sunny 16 rule** that states that an approximately-correct exposure will be obtained on a sunny day by using an aperture of f/16 and a shutter speed close to the reciprocal of the ISO speed of the film; for example, using ISO 200 film, an aperture of f/16, and a shutter speed of 1/200 second.

In a place with little light, for example, we could use a low value for the f/value (F/2.8) and a higher value for the shutter speed (for example 1/3). With these settings we won't be able to hold our camera steady for 1/3 second so the secret is to use a tripod, and if necessary, a delayed shutter, so that our fingers don't shake the camera when taking the photo.

Here's a photo of a studio wall covered with egg boxes, taken with these settings and a tripod:

This kept the actual room lighting pretty much the same, and the picture focused (except on the right, where the tips of the egg boxes were too close to the lens).

Size

When we buy a digital camera, we usually look at the maximum number of megapixels (millions of pixels, the elementary points of which a photo is comprised) of the photos it can take, but we should look at other things as well, such as the quality of the lens. "The bigger the better" is not always true, and in the case of digital photos, if we just want to make small prints or use them on our computer and on the Web, a size of 2 megapixels (1600x1200 pixels) is more than enough! If the main goal is this, then taking photos with 7 megapixels will be just silly—we'll need more space (this means more expensive camera cards to store photos, and bigger computer hard-disks), and more time to transfer the photos to our computer. Even 1600x1200 pixels is too much if we want, for example, to post one of these pictures in a forum post in Moodle—it would result in horizontal or vertical scrolling as the photo would be too big for a typical screen size. The best solution is to resize them to a proper width using an image editing software. Note that nowadays, it's hard to get just a 2 megapixels camera, but if we were to buy a 7 Megapixels camera, we can change the settings to take photos with just 2 Megapixels.

Enhancing pictures using GIMP

With photos, digital drawings, or pictures taken from the Web, we will need to crop, resize, rotate, correct, or compose them, so this will be the time to look at these common procedures. And we will do this with a free image editing software application called GIMP.

GIMP (http://www.gimp.org) is a cross-platform free software application for creating and modifying images and a nice alternative to commercial software such as Adobe Photoshop. With this tool, we can do various tasks, right from simple resize and crop operations to complex character drawing and photo editing. There are simple tools included in the Microsoft Windows as well, such as Paint or Picture viewer, that allow resizing and cropping. However, starting with GIMP to do these operations will get us used to the interface from the beginning of our course, so that later on we can do more complex operations such as photo editing.

At the time of writing this book, GIMP 1.2.2 is the latest release and hence all of the procedures used in this chapter refer to this release. The latest release may differ in terms of the GUI and may have some additional functionality.

After we download GIMP from `http://gimp.org/downloads` and install it, we will notice something different about this software as soon as we open it. There isn't a single window that contains several smaller windows, so if you are feeling a little bit confused, don't worry. After using it for some time, we will get used to it; really quickly!

The GIMP standard interface has five main elements as seen in the following screenshot:

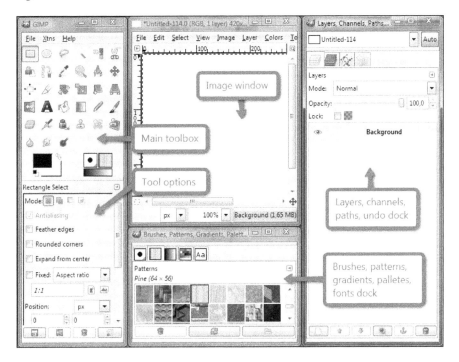

- **The main toolbox**: This is the heart of GIMP. It contains the highest-level menu, plus a set of icon buttons that can be used to select tools, and more. If you close it, GIMP closes.

- **Tool options**: Docked below the main **Toolbox** is a tool options dialog, showing options for the currently-selected tool (in the example above, the **Rectangle Select** tool).

- **An image window**: Each image opened in GIMP is displayed in a separate window. Many images can be open at the same time—the limit is set only by the amount of system resources. It is possible to run GIMP without having any images open, but there aren't many useful things to do in such a case.

- **Layers dialog**: This dialog window shows the layer structure of the currently-active image, and allows it to be manipulated in a variety of ways. It is possible to do a few very basic things without using the layers dialog, but even moderately sophisticated GIMP users will find it indispensable to have the layers dialog available at all times.

- **Brushes, Patterns, Gradients**: The docked dialog below the layer dialog shows the dialogs for managing brushes, patterns, and gradients.

Restoring GIMP's standard interface

Sometimes, by accident, we might close one of these elements. If this happens, in the **File** menu the Main Toolbox, select **Dialogs** and then **Create New Dock**, finally selecting the dock we closed:

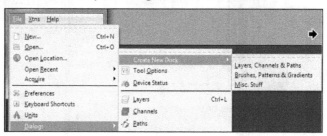

Cropping

In several modules of the course, Music for an everyday life, we will need to resize photos and screenshots so that they can be easily displayed in a Web browser in typical screen sizes, usually 1024x768 pixels. Let's work on an image from the Elephant's Dream movie, an open animation movie for which our students will have to create a movie trailer and add a soundtrack to, in *Module 3 – Music and Media*. This image will give the context to this activity and we will add it to the task description in the activity **Soundtrackers**. There is a problem though—the images available on the website of the movie, for example `http://download.blender.org/ED/cover.jpg`, are too large to fit a standard Moodle course page. If we added the image as-is, we would get something similar to the following:

The problem of using an image of this size in Moodle is obvious, so we will solve it by first cropping the image and then resizing it. We will crop the image because there's additional information in it that is not necessary for what we want, which is just to give some context to the activity. We will then resize it because it will be still too large to fit the course aptly.

So let's first open the original image in GIMP, after downloading it to our computer. For this we should:

1. Go to the **File** menu and click on **Open...**:

2. Select the picture that we saved to our computer, and click on **Open**:

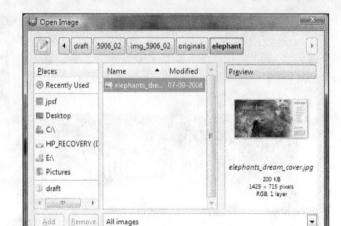

After the picture is opened in the image window, we will start by selecting the region of the picture that we want to crop using, of course, the **Crop Tool** in the main **Toolbox**. Don't forget that we can use the mouse to identify the functions of the buttons just by waiting a second with the mouse pointer over them. We are then ready to drag around the area we want. So, basically, for cropping:

1. Select the **Crop Tool** in the main **Toolbox**.
2. In the image window, left-click on the upper-left corner and with the mouse button held down, drag the mouse to the bottom right corner to the desired size (for example 1024x768). Don't worry if you are not being precise.
3. Double-click at the middle of the selected picture area.

Note that there will be a shaded part of the picture and this area will be cropped. Also note the squares at the corners of the selection. We can use these to adjust the crop area. When we double-click at the center of the selected area, we will obtain a picture similar to the following:

Resizing

The picture we cropped is still too large for our course (around 1000 pixels wide). As a result, before we insert it in our Soundtrackers activity, we will need to resize it. The HTML editor allows resizing of the photo but the problem is that the image loses quality. The best thing to do is resize it in GIMP. Now the obvious question would be: what works as a good size for Moodle courses? As a reference for the width of pictures in Moodle, we can use the following values (considering a typical screen size of 1024x768 and a standard theme):

Picture width	When to use
480 px	if the image is used inside a topic (as a topic title or label)
160 px	if the image is used inside a side block
640-800 px	if the image is used inside a Moodle resource or activity (for example, a forum post)

Resizing this image width to 640 px will make it look good in our course activity. The procedure to resize it is as follows:

1. From the top menu of the image window, click on **Image** and then **Scale Image...**:

2. Define a new **Width** value in the form (640 pixels in this case).

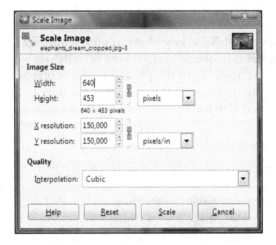

3. Click on the **Scale** button.

And the resize is done. Now, we just need to save it and upload it to our Moodle activity, and we will have something similar to the following screenshot:

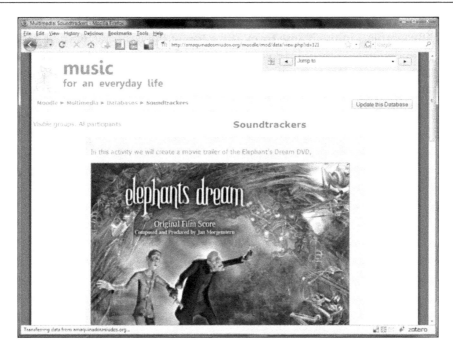

Saving

The original picture format of JPEG can be used in Moodle without great problems, so we will just need to save the cropped-then-resized version of our original. To do this, we should go to the **File** menu, and click on **Save As...**:

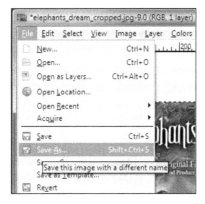

We can select the desired picture format using either of two methods in GIMP. The first is really simple — in the **Name** form at the top of the window, we just need to type the intended extension. GIMP will recognize this and convert the image to the desired format. In our case, we will keep the JPEG format so we will name the file **image_name.jpg**. GIMP will then recognize that we want to save the image in the JPEG format:

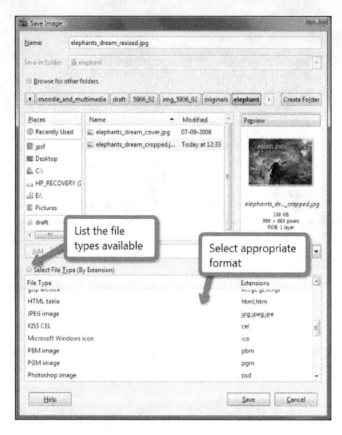

The second way to select the desired image format is through the interface. To do this , follow the steps below:

1. Go to the bottom of the **Save image** window, and click on the plus (**+**) button next to the text **Select File Type(By Extension)**.
2. Select the desired image format.
3. Select the destination folder in **Places**.
4. Click on the **Save** button.

And finally, after inserting the image in our Moodle activity Soundtrackers (using the HTML editor as we saw previously), we will get something similar to the following:

Rotating

Sometimes when we photograph a scene with a straight line on the background (the horizon is the best example but in a music studio the same can happen), if we are not using a tripod it's easy to get skewed photos. We can correct these mistakes in GIMP by using the **Rotate** tool, which is the button to the right of the **Crop** button in the **Toolbar**:

To rotate an image, we can do the following after opening the image file:

1. Select the **Rotate** tool from the **Toolbar**.

2. Click on the image.

3. A pop-up window will appear. We can use the slider to adjust the image or enter a value for the angle (negative values if you want to rotate the image counterclockwise).

4. Click on the **Rotate** button.

5. In the end, we can use the crop tool to eliminate areas of the photo that are missing.

Flipping and rotating

Flipping and rotating are very easy tasks to perform in GIMP. If we need to flip an image horizontally or vertically, or rotate it (for example, 90° clockwise) we just need to go to the **Layer** menu and click on **Transform** and select the required option from the submenu.

Correcting white balance and color

In situations with bad lighting, for example, incandescent light, we will need to correct the white balance, and in worse situations, the color balance of the photo. We can do this in the following three ways:

- Use the auto white balance function
- Adjust the levels
- Adjust the color balance

One quick alternative is to use the auto white balance function of GIMP. Go to **Colors | Auto | White Balance**:

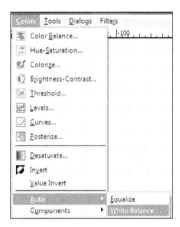

If the auto white balance doesn't do the trick, the second option is to use the levels tool. Go to **Colors | Levels...**. You can then use the eye dropper tool on the left in the **Levels** window to choose a point in the photo that is completely black and the one on the right for a completely white. If you can't get both points, try to get one and check the results.

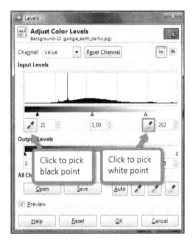

The third option is to use the color balance function. Go to **Colors | Color Balance...**. We can adjust the color levels and compensate for any lack or excess of a particular color, by selecting the range of colors (**Shadows, Midtones,** or **Highlights**) and using the slides for each of the color levels.

Correcting brightness and contrast

If the photos are over-exposed (there is extra light) we can reduce the brightness and compensate with the contrast to improve the quality. Select menu option **Colors | Brightness-Contrast...**. This can also be used to intensify the contrast of the photo, giving it well-defined shadows. However, note that when we use all of these options, the photo loses information and, if we are not careful, the resulting image can be worse than the original one.

We have now seen how to capture and enhance photos and images in general. Let's now see other useful actions that we can perform on pictures.

Let's see how we can make photo collages, a way of combining several images to make a new one, again using GIMP.

Creating digital photo collages

Photo collages are a great way to make posters, site headers, CD art, flyers, certificates, or storyboards. They basically consist of placing together parts from several pictures to make a new one. This can be done on paper of course, and then scanned or photographed to convert it to a digital format (try it, it's fun) or we can do the whole process digitally, using GIMP.

In our course, in *Module 7 – Music and the commons*, students are required to edit a CD made of music selections or their own music. In this CD, they will need to create a CD cover. This will be a good context to introduce the photo collage technique.

As we are combining different photos into a single one, we should create a folder to keep all of the photos and a project file. GIMP, besides saving in JPEG, PNG formats, and many others, also has one dedicated format for projects that contain several layers, called XCF. So as an example, I have created the following structure:

An important concept in photo collages is layers. Let's start with this concept.

Adding layers

Layers can be compared in some ways to audio and video projects, as kind of "tracks" where we can insert pictures and combine them in a final project.

The first thing to do in our photo collage is to get a nice background image, and at least one other image to work as a layer to add on top of the background. The procedure for adding layers is as follows:

1. Open the picture that we want to use as a background for the montage. (Menu option **File | Open** or *CTRL + O*.)

2. Make sure that the **Layers** dialog box is visible. (If it is not, we can select **Dockable Dialogs | Layers** or use the *CTRL + L* shortcut).

3. Open the picture that we want to combine with the first one (Select **File | Open** or *CTRL + O*). This will open a new window.

4. In this new window, select the picture (Menu option **Select | All** or *CTRL + A*).

5. Copy it to the clipboard (Menu option **Edit | Copy** or *CTRL + C*).

6. Click on the background image window.

7. Paste the picture (Menu option **Edit | Paste** or *CTRL + V*).

GIMP will automatically create a new layer called **Floating Selection (Pasted Layer)**, which can be seen in the **Layers** dialog box.

Sources: n/i (1983). p37f018.Retrieved September 22, 2008, from
http://www.jobim.org/xmlui/handle/2010/9432; n/i (n/d).
Tom Jobim.Retrieved September 22, 2008, from http://www.jobim.org/

We have to make sure that the photo we have pasted is smaller than the one in the background. Cropping or resizing it before this can be useful. However, it doesn't need to have the final size for publishing, as we will be able to resize it later, as a layer.

In the **Layers** dialog box, we can also change the name of the layers in our project , by double-clicking on one of the layers, which can be helpful if we have many.

Eliminating photo areas

It's a common procedure in photo collages to eliminate some of the photo's areas such as backgrounds, or cutting around the profile of a person to isolate them. We will use a technique called **Layer Mask** that will help us do this easily. To do this, first open the **Layers** dialog box and follow these steps:

1. Right-click on the layer we just created (floating selection).
2. Double-click on the **Floating Selection (Pasted Layer)** in the Layers dialog box and change the name of the layer (for example, for Layer 1). Select the **Add Layer Mask** option.
3. We are given some options, and the default ones are what we need — **White (full opacity)**. So let's click on **Add**.

We get something similar to the following, in the **Layers** dialog box:

Note that we can click either on the thumbnail of the picture or on the thumbnail of the mask (in white, to the right of the thumbnail). We should click on the latter to start removing the background.

To remove the background we need to select the Paintbrush tool in the **Toolbox**, with black as the foreground. When we start painting our foreground image in the selected areas, these will become transparent. To correct any mistakes, we should invert the foreground and background colors and paint with the brush in white, and the original image will return again. Control the zoom and the **Brush Scale** to get more or less detail.

Once we are done, we can scale this layer by going to **Layer | Scale Layer** (don't use the **Image | Scale**, as this will cause the entire image, including all layers, to be resized) and place it where we want it, by using the Move tool.

Adding text

Finally, let's add some text to it. Using the **Text Tool**, we can enter some text in the GIMP text editor. A new layer will be created for this.

In the tool options, we can select the **Font**, **Size**, and other attributes for the text.

Finally, let's add a drop shadow to the text, by going to **Filters | Light and Shadow | Drop Shadow**. An offset of 4 pixels and a blur radius of 5, with 50% opacity, and no resizing will be a good standard shadow for the text. You can experiment with these values and see the results.

The final result will be similar to the following image:

We can now save the file in XCF format to keep all of the layers information
(**File | Save as**). After that, we can save it in a more usable format for the Web, such
as PNG, and publish it on Moodle, for example as a forum attachment with ratings.
Several CD covers proposed by students can be voted and the winner selected.

Capturing screenshots

Capturing screenshots can be very useful if we are:

- Creating a "how to" document on using a computer application and we need to illustrate the procedures
- Creating a presentation about some online resources and showing how they look (assuming that we don't have an Internet connection during the presentation)
- Getting some frames from a video (for example, a DVD or a Web based video)
- Keeping records of webshots (website screenshots) that we find interesting, in order to post on our blog or in Moodle (for example, a portfolio of some websites that we have developed)

We can take screenshots in one of the following two ways:

- By using the **Print Screen** function supported by the majority of computers (and keyboards) to capture the entire screen or a specific application window, and then save it as an image using GIMP
- By using **Jing** (`http://www.jingproject.com/`) to directly capture a region of the screen (and insert callouts on it, such as the screenshots used in this book!)

Now it's time to create our first window capture. Let's start with the first technique, that is, using the *Print screen* key and GIMP.

Capturing screenshots by using the Print Screen key

In the final course module, to wrap up, we will require students to create a digital portfolio of their best works from the course. This will involve capturing screenshots of some of the products of the course and later creating a voice thread where they have to comment on these screenshots (we will see how to create these voice threads in Chapter 5). For now, we will look at an example of a screenshot of an online map that students had to build in *Module 2 - Music evolves*, showing the location of some instruments on a world map and some of its characteristics.

The steps for a screen capture are as follows:

1. Prepare the window on the desktop that we want to capture. In this case it will be a browser window opened on our map.
2. Press on the *Print Screen* key, and capture the entire screen.

3. Open GIMP, go to **File | Acquire** and click on **Paste as New** (or use the key combination *Shift + CTRL + V*). An image window will open, containing the captured screenshot that we can now edit and save. Note that you could use this paste option in other kind of applications, such as a word processor, usually using the common paste function or *CTRL+V* key combination.

The captured screenshot will look similar to the following:

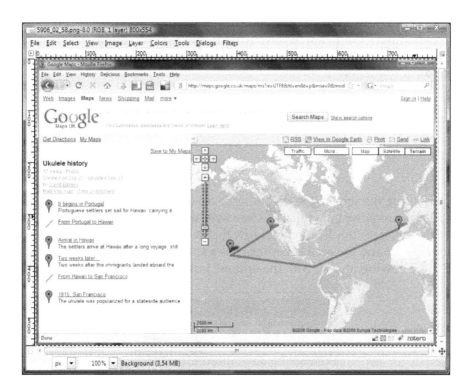

There is a method of capturing just the application window that we want, instead of a full screen. This can be helpful if we don't want the application window maximized (for example, if we want less white space in a webpage to be shown). We can use a shortcut for this, pressing the *CTRL + ALT + Print Screen* keys simultaneously. Again in GIMP, we just need to go to **Acquire | Paste as New** to save the result.

In both cases, there are some issues that we should consider before taking a screenshot. One of the first things you need to bear in mind is that if you want to use the screenshot in a Web page or document, it should have an appropriate size. For this, we should reduce the window sizes and elements that we want to capture and fit them to standard sizes adequate to our medium, minimizing all of the empty space, and increasing the letter size if necessary. To have a look at copyright issues concerning screenshots, refer to Chapter 8.

Capturing screenshots using Jing

Jing (http://www.jingproject.com) is a screen capture software application that allows us to take screenshots (commented like the ones in this book, or not) and screen videos (with our own voice, for example explaining procedures for a piece of software. These desktop recordings are usually called screencasts (and we will see how to make them in Chapter 4) and can be made in both Mac and Microsoft Windows (sorry Linux users, you can find several alternatives such as vnc2swf, xvidcap, recordmydesktop, and so on). After installing and running it, we can access it through a "sunny" interface that we can access and move anytime and anywhere on the desktop.

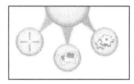

To start capturing the screen, the first thing to do we is to click on the left-most button (after positioning the mouse pointer over the sun) and then selecting the region of the screen or application window that we want to capture. When we do this, the frame around the area to capture has a small menu on its bottom left corner (refer to the following image) with the options **Image**, **Video**, **Redo**, and **Cancel**:

Clicking on the **Image** button reveals some of the advantages of Jing over the previous technique of using the Print Screen key. The first one is that it allows us to comment directly on the captured image, giving us a set of tools to do it:

To cancel a capture, we just need to click the right mouse button or select something and then click on the **Cancel** button. Once we have selected an area to capture, we can save it by clicking on the **Save** button in the publishing options. Note that we can publish the screenshots directly to our Flickr account (for example), by adding a customized button (click on the last button in the publishing options and explore!).

One of Jing's limitations is that if we take a capture, comment it, and save it, we cannot correct or change what we did in the exported file, so we will have to create a new commented screenshot.

Creating comic strips using Strip Generator

Comics are a great way of telling a story. They can be used to:

- Create hypothetical situations that could happen in real life (for example, a conflict or a funny situation)
- Create a storyboard for a movie
- Narrate an event

If you are getting worried that we will have to draw something and your skills are, well, those of a 10 year old kid, that's not a problem, as mine aren't that good either! Fortunately, there's a tool just for you and me, called **Strip Generator**, which will save us from further humiliation in front of our students and colleagues. In our course in Moodle, in *Module 5 – Being a musician*, we will design an activity where students have to create a story based on a day in the life of a musician, and they will be required to use this tool to illustrate this. As we will be using a comic strip, we will be drawing the results in an image. We can then add this work to the Moodle course easily, as an attachment to a forum.

Strip generator (`http://stripgenerator.com/`) is an online tool for creating comic strips with an easy-to-use drag-and-drop interface that makes creating comics look simple.

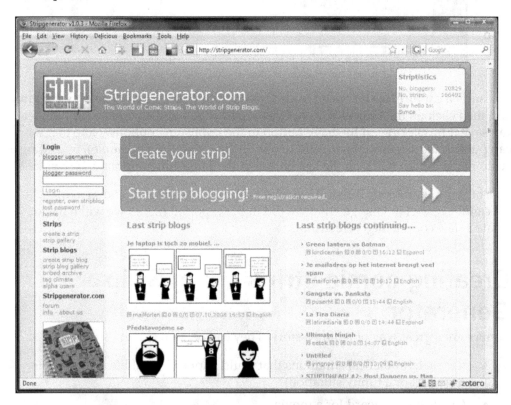

You can see some of the examples that other comic strip "artists" did by going to the strip blog gallery or by searching on some keywords. Here's one as an example, about a lesson in sharing:

Source: fanton (2007, April 26). A lesson in sharing. Retrieved October 17, 2009, from
`http://welcometocartoon.stripgenerator.com/2007/04/26/a-lesson-in-sharing.html`

Adding elements

To start a comic strip, we'll first have to create an account. Once you are done with that, click on the **create a strip** link under the **Strips** heading on the left-side of the menu.

We are then presented with the following workspace to start building the comic strip:

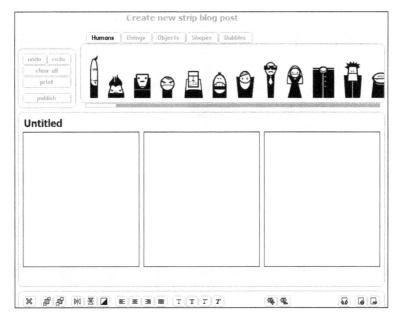

On the top, we can select characters, objects, shapes, and bubbles. The three white rectangles (frames) are actually where we will make our story, by dragging the elements from the top into them. Note that we can't upload any pictures, so we are limited to the elements provided.

The editing tools in the toolbar below the three frames allow us to delete elements, send them to the back of other elements, flip, format text in bubbles, zoom in or out, and so on. We just need to hover the mouse over these buttons to see their functions.

When we add an element to a frame, we can also move, resize, or rotate it, by either dragging it around, or by using the small circles on the object's boundary.

Publishing

After we are done creating a comic strip, we just have to follow these steps to publish it to Moodle:

1. Click on **Publish**. If we don't do this and navigate away from the page, we might lose all of our work!
2. Give a title to the strip, and click the **Save** button.
3. Fill in the form field to **Create new strip blog post**. Add some tags, define the language of the strip, and describe its content.

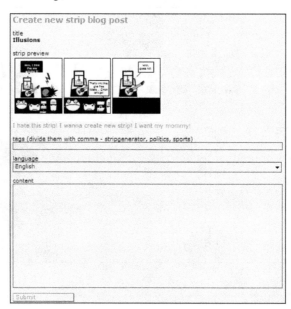

Strip generator uses a blog mechanism to publish our comic strips. After we post it, we see the final result, and if we click on it, a window appears with information for linking and embedding as seen in the following screenshot:

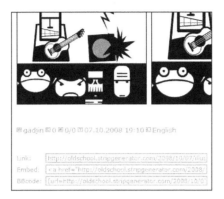

As this comic strip is an image, we can also save it by right-clicking on the image (comic strip) and selecting the **Save image as...** option. Finally, we can upload it as an attachment to our forum activity, as seen in the following screenshot:

Now that we know how to create comic strips, let's have a look at some basic procedures that we can execute, to integrate presentations into our courses.

Creating slideshows

Slideshows are a great way of presenting information and supporting discussions; so we will have a look at the following things that can be useful in Moodle courses:

- How to convert PowerPoint slides to images, in order to integrate them in a Moodle lesson
- How to share our presentations through an online service called **Slideshare**, and then embed our presentations in Moodle
- How to create photo slideshows on the Web to later embed them in a Moodle resource or activity

Exporting PowerPoint slides as images to build Moodle lessons

An easy way to create an exercise in our Moodle courses is to build a lesson around a presentation that we used in class, for example, in Microsoft PowerPoint. This will provide the content, and then we can add some questions, working with the existing material and not having to rebuild it again in the Moodle lesson. The easiest way to do this is to convert the PowerPoint (or similar) presentation to images and then add these images to branch tables or question pages in our lesson.

The problem with this is that the image width of standard slides will be 960 pixels, a little bit large, as we saw, for a Moodle course. To overcome this problem (without having to resize each image in GIMP), after opening the presentation we should change the slide width and height before exporting them as images. We can do this by going to the **Design** tab and clicking on the **Page Setup** option as shown in the following screenshot:

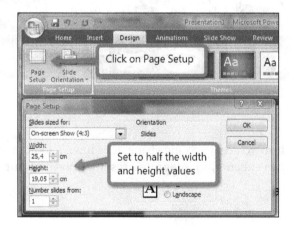

By setting both values to half of their current values (in cm, check the conversion table below to get the equivalent pixels), we will get images with a width of 480 pixels, which is a good size for inserting it in a lesson. If this size makes the text in the slides look too small we can use a width of 640 pixels. So, we would use the following values:

Desired width (pixels)	Width (cm)	Height (cm)
480	9,52	12,7
640	12,7	16,93

So now we are ready to export our presentation, by opening the presentation and then going to **File | Save as | Other Formats**, as seen in the following screenshot:

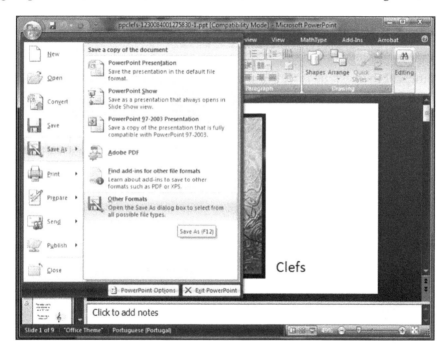

In the following window, insert a **File name** and select the **JPEG** option under **Save as type**:

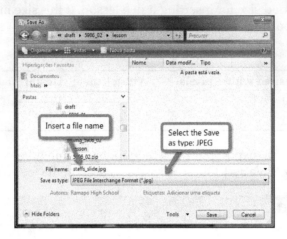

PowerPoint will then ask us if we want to save **Every Slide** or the **Current Slide Only**. In our case, we will be choosing the first option:

After this, a folder will be created with the same name as the **File name** that we have defined previously (`staffs_slide`) and the images of our slides will be saved inside this folder:

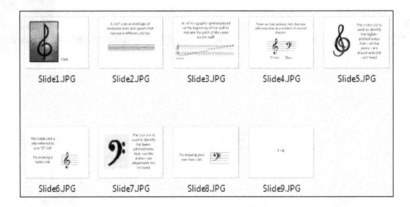

When inserting one of these images in a branch table in our Moodle lesson, we will get something similar to the following:

One drawback of this technique is accessibility, as the text in the images will not be read by screen readers. A possible solution for this is to add a good **Alternate text** to the images when inserting them using the HTML editor in Moodle.

Publishing presentations using Slideshare

Slideshare (`http://www.slideshare.net`) is an online service for sharing presentations. It is a good place to look for presentations for our courses. It's also a place where we can upload our presentations and make them available to many people in Flash format. Another advantage is that if we don't have a good upload limit in our Moodle course, we can add the presentation here and then embed it in our course!

To publish a presentation to Slideshare, we just need to create an account (and not even this if we don't want to publish) and upload our presentation (which can be in Microsoft PowerPoint, PDF, or OpenOffice formats). Slideshare will convert it to Flash and generate the code necessary to put our presentation anywhere on the Web.

So, let's upload the presentation by clicking on the **Browse and select files...** button:

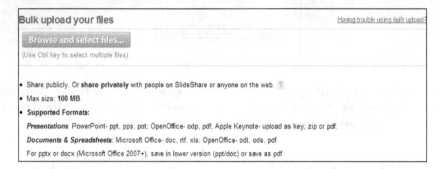

We need to navigate to and select the file that we want to upload. A progress bar will inform us of the file transfer, and when completed, we are required to fill in a form with some details about the presentation:

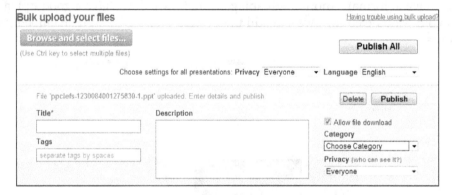

Note that we can allow or disallow the original file download. After we click on the **Publish** button, it will take some time to convert the file to Flash, and when it's ready, we can then get the **Embed** code required to add it to our Moodle course:

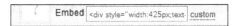

In *Module 7 – Music and the commons*, a presentation made available through this service is used as a starting point:

Creating online photo slideshows

Slide (http://www.slide.com) is a web application that allows us to create photo slideshows either using the images uploaded from our computer or from images that are already on the web (in services such as Flickr). And we don't need to install any software! This can be helpful in our course *Module 5 – Being a musician*, where students have to create a photo story of their favorite artist.

We will take a look at the basics of Slide, as it has many design options.

The editing area of the slideshow allows us to **Add images**, **Define styles** (and other design characteristics), and preview the result:

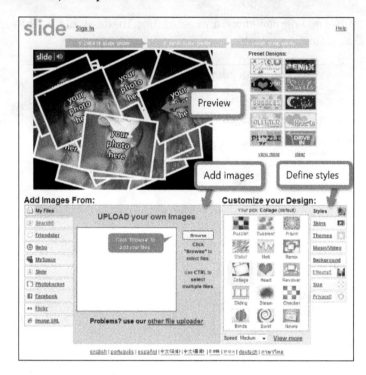

In the **Add images** area, we can start by uploading images from our computer (by clicking on the **Browse** button), add images from online services such as Flickr, or even add an image URL directly. When we add images, we can see the captions in the interface and rearrange them by dragging and dropping:

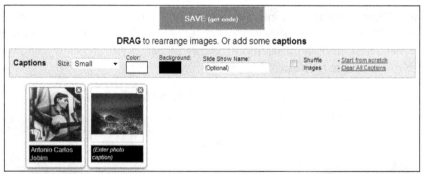

Sources: armatoj (2008, July 18). Antonio Carlos Jobim. Retrieved October 18, 2008, from http://www.flickr.com/photos/armatoj/2590347321/; Phillie Casablanca (2007, November 21). View of Rio de Janeiro. Retrieved October 18, 2008, from http://www.flickr.com/photos/philliecasablanca/2052845336/

After we have all of the captions ready and in order, the next step is to click on the **Save** button. We are then required to fill in a form with the **Slideshow Details**:

When we click the **SAVE Slideshow** button, we can then get the code to add the slideshow to Moodle. For this, we should select the last option on the left (**can't find what you're looking for? Try here!**) and then copy the code to the clipboard, pasting it into a Moodle form, later.

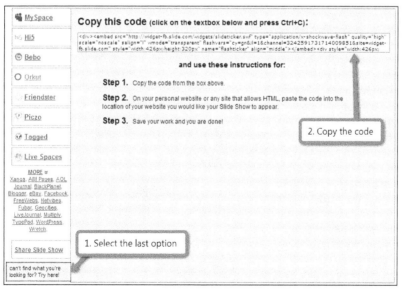

Sources of the captions: http://flickr.com/photos/philliecasablanca/2052059147 (13/02/09) and http://flickr.com/photos/armatoj/2590347321 (13/02/09) - CC by

Summary

In this chapter, we started by seeing how to find free pictures online to add to our course materials (and assignments, from a students' perspective) in services such as Flickr and Wikimedia Commons. We then had a look at different ways of inserting images in Moodle, especially using the HTML editor image upload function. We then started using GIMP for main image editing tasks, such as cropping, resizing, capturing (together with some photography concepts), color correction, photo collage, and saving the images in different formats. Some issues regarding images in Moodle, such as file formats and appropriate sizes, were also discussed, and we used the Print Screen function and Jing to collect screenshots. Strip generator was also used to easily create comic strips. We also learned how to export PowerPoint presentations to images, adding them to a Moodle lesson, or as an alternative publishing these presentations in Slideshare. We concluded this chapter by looking at ways to create photo slideshows using Slide.

3
Sound and Music

This chapter focuses on creating and editing sound and music for the course Music for an everyday life. This involves finding free audio online, creating our own voice recordings, remixing audio, podcasting, and even converting text to speech.

By the end of this chapter you will be able to:

- Use a set of free software tools for common procedures in sound and music editing
- Extract audio from CDs
- Create voice recordings
- Integrate all of the above into Moodle
- Select appropriate audio formats and settings according to your needs

Finding free music and sounds online

As with pictures, the usual suspect for finding free audio tracks online is again Wikimedia Commons. This is a huge database of multimedia elements, and we can find interesting stuff there. But before we look into these, let's start with the basics of audio formats so that we can pick better files for our courses.

The basics of audio formats

In our everyday life, we can find music and sound in several formats. The most common of these formats are:

- **PCM**: This is the standard format used in CDs. It is a uncompressed audio format, which implies large file sizes—around 10MB per minute.
- **WAV**: WAV is usually used to store the PCM file format. It can contain audio in several rates and bitrates (these are concepts that we will see in a moment).

- **MP3**: MPEG Layer 3 is one of the most common audio formats on the Web. It is also the name of the codec that reduces original audio files sizes (for example, depending on the bitrate and rate, a CD track can be reduced to 1/10th the size of the original file size).

- **WMA**: Windows Media Audio; this is the standard audio format released by Microsoft.

- **OGG**: An open source file format that can contain several codecs, Vorbis being the most common.

- **MIDI**: The MIDI format is an industry standard for electronic music, allowing electronic musical instruments, computer software, and other equipments to communicate. For example, a MIDI keyboard uses MIDI to communicate with a computer. You have probably heard a MIDI file before, usually a very small sized file, that sounds as electronic music from the 80's (yes, they were used quite a lot in those crazy times). However, as MIDI files don't actually have audio waveforms in them, it is possible to associate real instrument sounds to MIDI instructions and have nice sounding files.

There are four concepts to keep in mind when dealing with audio files (and video files, as we will see in the next chapter) namely file format, codec, rate, and bitrate.

The file format is the easy one—whatever extension a file has, that is its file format, for example, MP3, WAV, OGG, and so on. The codec does the processing of the data inside the file, for example, in OGG it can use the Vorbis audio codec.

In addition to these two, rate and bitrate refer to the number of times per second that an original audio is sampled and stored in Hz, the same as 1/s, and the number of bits that are processed in every unit of time (Kb/s) respectively.

I would recommend MP3 as a working format for our daily needs (in Moodle or anywhere else), in which we can use different rates and bitrates according to our goal for example, make a song excerpt from a CD available or add voice to forums. Check the following table for some reference values:

Rate	Bitrate	When to use
44100 Hz	128 Kb/s	To rip CDs and use in most cases
11025 Hz	48 Kb/s	To record voice for a daily use (interviews, students answers, comments, and so on)

Now that we know this, let's start by finding free sound tracks and free music on the Web for our audio projects.

Internet Archive: Audio archive

The Internet Archive (http://www.archive.org) is an online library that provides permanent access to historical material on the Web, to save it as "memory". We can see this in action, for example, in the **Wayback Machine** (http://www.archive.org/web/web.php), where we have access to static versions of web pages from their start to the present day, with some of the archiving occurring as old as 1996 (this can be a really fun activity!). One of the sub-projects of this initiative is the Audio Archive (http://www.archive.org/details/audio), a library with over 300,000 free digital recordings, ranging from old radio shows to concerts and poetry readings.

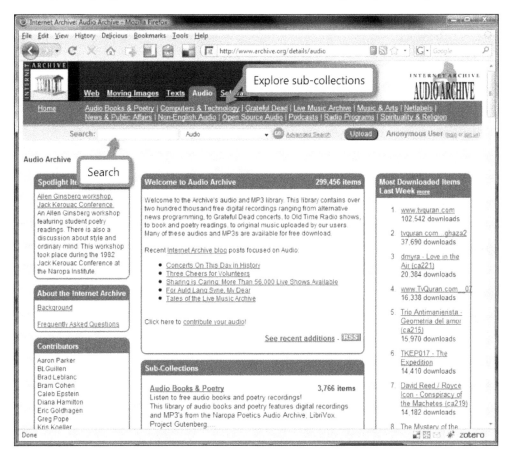

We can either search this collection using the **Search** form or explore the sub-collections.

Freesound

Freesound (`http://www.freesound.org`) is a collaborative collection of sounds licensed under a Creative Commons license, allowing us to use them in our own works.

CCMixter

CCMixter (`http://ccmixter.org`) is a project from the Creative Commons initiative where we can find lots of samples to use in our audio projects. We can also upload the results to the same site. All of the content is licensed under Creative Commons licenses.

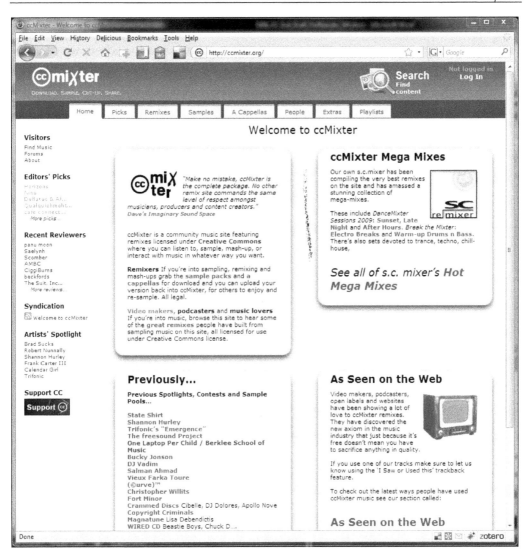

Imeem

Imeem (`http://www.imeem.com`) is a community for music sharing where we can find and upload music, create playlists, and embed them in Moodle (and other websites).

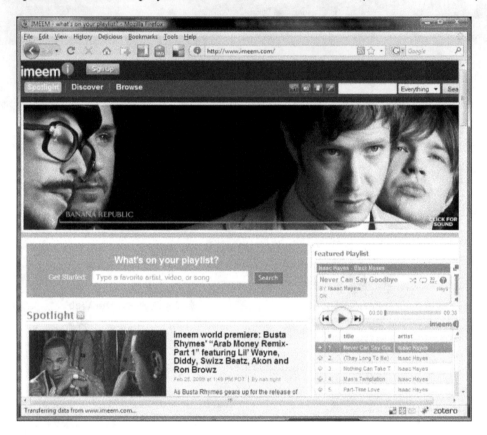

If we search for a song using the **Search** form, we are taken to a page where we can get a player and an embed code that we can use to embed the song in our Moodle course. Here's an example, using a song by **Radiohead** from their album "In Rainbows":

We can now have a look at how to upload audio and create playlists in Imeem—something that can be used easily in our course in order to give it some musicality! And this doesn't mean that we can only use this for music-related courses. Every course is a good course to have music on!

Uploading audio to Imeem

Uploading in Imeem is easy. We just need to follow these steps:

1. After creating an account in Imeem, navigate to the **Dashboard**. Click on the **Upload** button in the top menu:

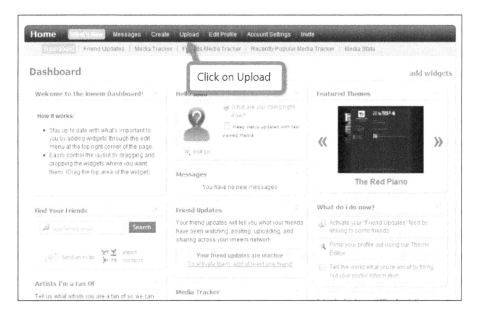

2. In the next window that we are presented with, click on **Web Uploader**.

3. Select the options **Upload Music** and **Put it on my Profile**, and click on the **Upload** button:

4. Follow the steps to upload files from the computer (there are four straight-forward steps, consisting of selecting the music tracks, uploading, editing music information, and finishing the upload):

The uploaded files will be listed on the **Recent Uploads** page, as shown in the following screenshot:

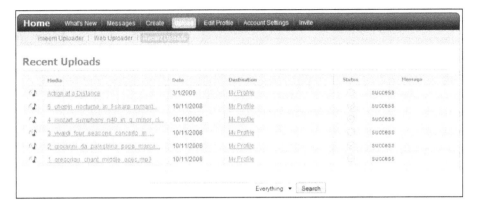

Creating playlists in Imeem

Instead of having just one song embedded in our Moodle course, we can have an entire sequence of songs, called playlist. To create a playlist from our uploads (or from the list of songs made available by other users), in the top menu, we should select **Create | Music Playlist**. Next, right-click on your user name and then click on **New Playlist**.

We are presented with a modal box as seen in the following screenshot. We must enter a **Title** (in this case **Classical**) and a brief **Description** of the playlist finally clicking the **Save** button.

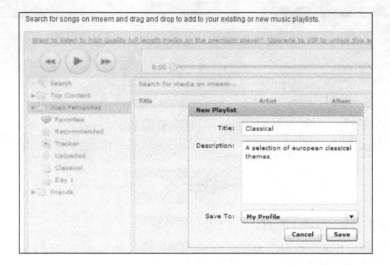

In the left-hand menu, if we click on **Uploaded**, we will get access to our uploaded files. We can then drag and drop these files (songs) to your playlist, which can also be seen the left-side of the menu. If we want to add other songs that we did not upload yourself, we just have to perform a search, and then drag and drop the result to our playlist in the same way.

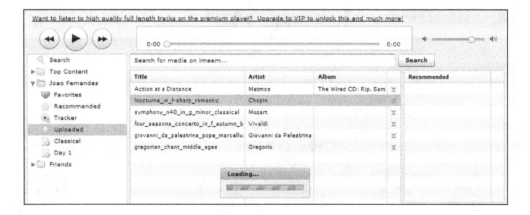

After the playlist has all of the songs that you want we can see the following screenshot:

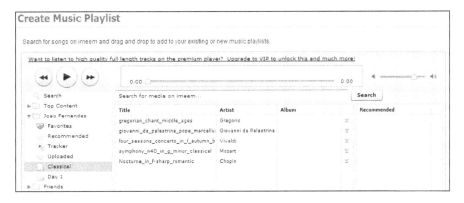

Now to get the embed code to add the playlist to Moodle, right-click on the playlist **Classical** and select the **View Playlist** option:

The playlist will be displayed, and we can copy the embed code:

In our course, all of the songs were added in every module's delivery moment, to have students' experience different music styles and artists:

A playlist was also added to a side block on the main course page, as a kind of "course soundtrack":

Other music and sound sites

In addition to the services that we saw above, we can also find music and sounds for free at:

- Musopen (http://www.musopen.com): An online music library of public domain music
- Magnatune (http://www.magnatune.com): A new way of selling music, where we can listen to the songs for free first!
- Odeo (http://www.odeo.com): An online service with lots of music, including an education section
- Soundsnap (http://www.soundsnap.com): A database of sound loops

Before we get into the details of how to create audio for our course, let's have a quick look at how we can integrate audio into Moodle.

Moodle it!

To integrate audio into Moodle, we have two options:

- Upload an audio file to the course's files area and then link to it by using any HTML editor — if Moodle has the multimedia filter working, and if we are talking about MP3 files, a flash player will automatically be inserted to play the file. We have seen this in Chapter 1.

 The flash player in Moodle only accepts MP3 files with a sample rate of 11.025, 22.050, or 44.100 kHz, a bitrate below 128 Kbps, and preferably **CBR (Constant Bit Rate)** over **VBR (Variable Bit Rate)**. Usually, you won't have problems, but if you hear a chipmunk-like sound when you play one of these files in Moodle the problem will probably be in one of these properties.

- Upload an audio file to an online service and then embed it in Moodle — this is what we have done in Imeem.

The same applies to other audio formats recognized by the multimeda plugin in Moodle (in audio, Real Player for now, in video others such as Windows Media Player or Apple Quicktime). In this case, we will need to have the players installed in our computer and these will be embedded in the Moodle course. But the easiest one is MP3 as we just need the Flash plug-in. We can convert any audio to MP3 using Audacity, a tool we will explore in a moment. So now that we have the sources for our raw materials, let's have a look at how we can build on the work of others and create our own audio.

Creating and delivering

A long time ago, I put together two radio shows, with a friend of mine, for a radio station in Caldas, a nice place north of Lisbon, Portugal. A friend of a friend owned the place. He was an entrepreneur who enjoyed taking risks (he didn't even know us well and we hadn't done any prior work in that area). As my memory is terrible, I can't remember the titles of the shows, I just remember that we joked about the 80's and 90's, using themes from TV and movie shows (such as the Knight Rider, Baywatch, and Soldiers of Fortune), and included some sketches with strange characters and weird dialogues and, of course, some nice sound effects that we got for free from the Web. I don't remember him inviting us for a third show, but at the time he and the team laughed a lot and we certainly had a great time doing it. The same happened for jazz themes (and some originals — scary to have this recorded for a son or daughter to listen to later!) that we played with some friends, in our egg-box home-made studio, using a minidisc and a microphone.

In school, as a teacher, most of the work that I did in audio, with students had to do with soundtracks for small movies, combining, for example, voice and music for a documentary about a nature reserve (the Sado river, near Lisbon, a beautiful place). They voted for the best voice, after some auditions and recordings, and picked some of the songs for the soundtrack, later combining them into groups by using Windows Movie Maker as a draft. Later on, their work was used in Adobe Premiere and Encore, to make a proper DVD. These are some examples of what we can do with audio, but there are many others, such as:

- Radios (online or regular) and all sorts of programs
- Interviews
- Critiques or commentaries of CDs, songs, movies, books, or articles
- Music CDs, podcasts
- Audio-books
- Video soundtracks
- Discussions in Moodle forums with voice or instruments' recordings

Let's start off with a simple task, that is, by extracting audio from CDs.

Extracting audio from CDs using VLC

When teaching several subjects, particularly related to music and language, audio can be extremely useful, almost mandatory. We can give students the opportunity to listen to interviews, stories, audio-books, dialogues, music, even their own voices. More than that, we can give them the opportunity to create all of these on their own.

One of our course modules will be dedicated to Music and Media, and one of the main tasks in this module, the activity Soundtrackers, will be to create a soundtrack for a movie trailer of Elephants Dream (something we saw in the previous chapter, when cropping and resizing pictures). This soundtrack will be made by students from songs and sound effects. Let's first focus on the music, and see how we can extract audio from **The Wired CD** (http://creativecommons.org/wired) as an example:

Note that we are using a CD that is not copyright protected for this task. These instructions will still work with most copyright protected CDs (which include most CDs that you buy), but be careful that you are not breaking any laws by doing so. Please have a look at Chapter 8 for some advice on this.

VLC Media Player (`http://www.videolan.org/vlc`) is a free, cross-platform media player that can play almost any available media file. This can be very important for video, as there is an incredible variety of video codecs that are available these days (divx, xvid, h.264, vc-1, and so on), encapsulated in many container formats (avi, mp4, asf, wmv, mov, and so on) . But before we get to work with video, let's start with something simpler—that is, audio.

VLC can be used to play and extract audio from a CD. Audio CDs have been available since 1982 and are used to store music by using a technique called PCM encoding. However, we will use the MP3 format in our Moodle course for several reasons:

- The files have smaller sizes
- Moodle has a MP3 filter that automatically puts a player in place so that we can listen to the song without downloading it, simply by clicking on the play button
- MP3-format songs are easy to edit, and to create podcasts from, because MP3 has become the standard for sound and music files

We will first convert some of the tracks of this audio CD to MP3 files on our hard disks. This is what we call ripping. So first, let's put the Wired CD in the CD player of our computer and choose the tracks for our soundtrack.

At the time of writing this book, VLC Media Player 0.8.7 is the latest release and hence all of the procedures used in this chapter refer to this release. The latest release may differ in terms of the GUI and may have some additional functionality.

Ripping a CD track

VLC has a wizard that is helpful in defining the settings to rip the CD track to an MP3 format.

1. Open the VLC media player and go to **File | Wizard...**.
2. Select the **Transcode/Save to file** option.
3. Click on the **Next** button, as shown in the following screenshot:

In the next window, we need to define the input (the source that we are going to rip), in this case the specific audio CD track. So, click on the **Choose...** button:

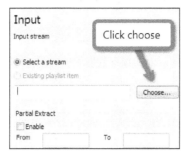

Now it's time to select the track to rip:

1. Click on the **Disc** tab.

2. Select **Audio CD** in the **Disc type** field.

3. Enter the audio track number in the **Track** field.

4. Click on the **OK** button.

VLC should then take us back to the **Input** window, with the audio track already selected (under **Select a stream**, in my case this is **cdda://E:@1** — the **E:** refers to the CD drive in my computer and hence, it may vary), so we just need to click on the **Next** button.

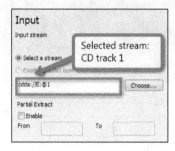

We now have to select the destination audio codec in the **Transcode** window, so we should select the **Transcode audio** checkbox and then select the MP3 codec, with a bitrate of 128 kb/s (the frequency of the PCM original file, 44100Hz, will be retained) as we saw in the table of reference values in this chapter.

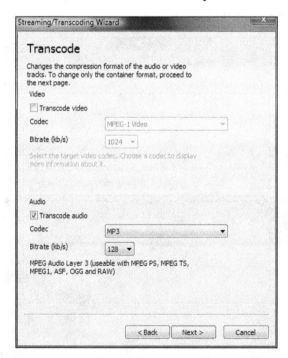

After clicking **Next**, the **Encapsulation format** window is displayed. Here, we should leave the default of **RAW** as the selection. After clicking on the **Next** button again, we need to choose where to save the file:

1. Click on the **Choose** button.
2. Browse to the destination folder.
3. Add a file name and specify the file extension **.mp3**.
4. Click on the **Save** button.

Finally, after we click on the **Finish** button, the transcoding will start and the wizard will disappear. The VLC player will look the same, and although nothing appears to be happening, the transcoding process is working in the background. We can recognize this in two ways—by listening to your CD drive working (if it's working, the transcoding is still going on) or by looking at the status bar at the bottom of the VLC media player window, as shown in the screenshot below:

When the time values are static, it's done. Now that we have some audio to work with, it's time to start the editing!

Creating and editing audio using Audacity

Audacity (`http://audacity.sourceforge.net`) is a free software utility for audio recording and editing, that works on several platforms. It can be used to make high-quality recordings with a microphone (or other sources), easy editing and mixing of different sounds, mixing speech and music just like a real radio station, adding different audio effects, and all of this using a multi-track interface, where each audio file is assigned to a different track, which is a kind of layer that we can edit individually. The majority of the music that we listen to is recorded using this multi-track method, meaning that each instrument is recorded separately and then merged into a single audio file for playback.

At the time of writing this book, Audacity 1.2.7 is the latest release and hence all of the procedures used in this chapter refer to this release. The latest release may differ in terms of the GUI and may have some additional functionality.

We will now see how we can use Audacity for some common procedures in audio creation and editing, such as:

- Slicing a track
- Capturing audio from a microphone
- Remixing audio

Audacity's interface has six main areas:

- **The control toolbar**: This has the most important tools for editing the audio tracks and controlling the playback and recording.
- **The meter toolbar**: This indicates the input and output levels, so that we can get a visual indication of the levels, for example, if your microphone is very low or if the final sound is too high.
- **The mixer toolbar**: This has the control sliders for the output level (a standard volume indicator) and your input level (for example, increasing the volume of the microphone before or during the recording).
- **The editor toolbar**: This has the tools for cutting, copying, and pasting selections, in addition to trimming, silence generation, undo and redo, and zooming.
- **The timeline**: This indicates the length of the recording or playback, in minutes and seconds.
- **The tracks**: These are the different sounds that are a part of the audio project.

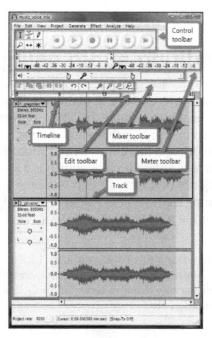

Let's start with the basic operation of slicing music tracks.

Slicing a track

Continuing our work in creating a soundtrack for the Elephants Dream movie trailer, the next step is to create slices of the music tracks that we extracted from the Wired CD. As we want to create a limited video excerpt, we couldn't fit the entire music tracks so we will have to cut out the parts that we don't want. This slicing is also useful in *Module 1 – Music evolves*, where students have to create short audio clips from several music eras, and post them as attachments in forum posts.

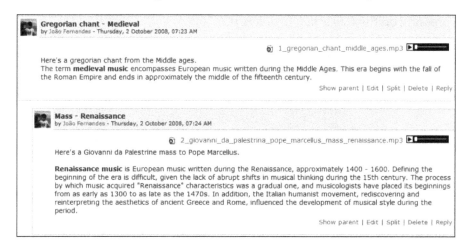

For slicing, we should start by creating a new audio project.

Creating a new audio project

To create audio clips from larger music files, the first thing to do is to create a new audio project. This means that we will have a folder where we can keep all of our files. So after opening Audacity, go to the **File** menu and then click on **Save project as...** and select a destination folder. A project file with the .AUP extension will be created (in my case I called it **music_selection**) and a sub-folder (**music_selection_ data**) will automatically be created by Audacity to contain all of the changes that we make to the original files. It's a good idea to create a folder, in the destination folder, for the original music files that we will be using in the soundtrack project (I have called it **music**). Hence, the folder structure will look similar to the following:

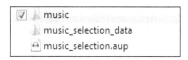

Importing audio

The first part of the slicing process consists of importing a music file into the workspace as a track. We call this importing audio, and we need to go to the **File** menu and click on **Import | Audio...**, selecting the original music file (in MP3 format by now in our music folder) and then clicking on **OK**.

Selecting and deleting track parts

We have two options for deleting the parts of the music file that we are not interested in. The first is to use the **Selection tool** in the control toolbar, and then, with the mouse drag the mouse over the selection of the waveform that we wish to delete, finally pressing on the *Delete* key to delete it.

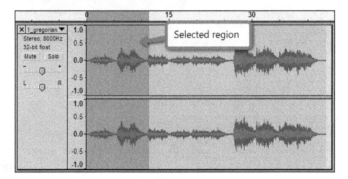

The second method is ideal for selecting an excerpt from the middle of the music file. In this method we use the **Trim** tool, which is below the **Selection** tool in the editor toolbar. This will remove the audio regions before and after the excerpt that we select.

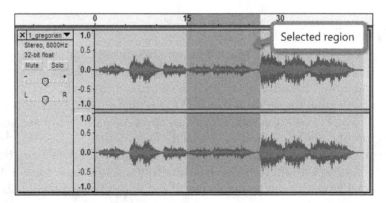

We shouldn't worry about the empty spaces before and after the file, if we use the second option.

Fading in and fading out

If we remove parts of the track at the beginning and/or end of the music file, it can happen that if we play it now (using the control bar play button or the *Space* key), it starts and ends abruptly. Audacity has an option to make these smoother—the fade in and out effects.

To use these effects, we will first have to select a portion of the beginning of the excerpt, usually around three seconds. We can see this duration in the timeline and set it to more or less by using the **Zoom** tool. Then, after selecting around three seconds of music, select menu option **Effect | Fade In,** and it's done for this part. We should apply the same principles to the end of the excerpt, in this case using the **Fade Out** effect.

Exporting to MP3

Due to copyright issues, Audacity cannot export audio files to the MP3 format out-of-the-box, so we will need to install an MP3 encoder called LAME, which is available free of cost:

1. Go to the LAME MP3 Encoder download page at `http://lame.buanzo.com.ar`.

2. Save the ZIP file for our OS to your computer and unzip it. It should contain the `lame_enc.dll` file. We should keep this file in a folder that we will not accidentally delete.

3. Open up Audacity. Go to the **Edit | Preferences...** and in the **Quality** tab, set the **Default rate** to 44100 Hz (CD quality) and the **Bit Rate** to **128** Kbps on the **File Formats** tab. Also, in the **MP3 Export Setup under** the **File Formats** tab, click on the **Find library** button and select the `lame_enc.dll` file to allow Audacity to export files in the MP3 format (you will only need to do this once). After doing this, click on the **OK** button to go back to the project.

Finally, we should export our music selection to an MP3 file, by going to **File | Export as MP3...** and specifying some of the ID3v1 tags. Our files will then be ready to Moodle! Note two things about this:

- We can use this procedure to convert another audio format to MP3, first opening it in Audacity and then exporting to MP3.

- To save MP3 audio files with other rates and bitrates (for example, voice recordings), we should first change the above values and then export the result.

Capturing audio from a microphone (line in)

Capturing audio from a microphone (or any other input device) can be useful for many activities, such as:

- Adding audio comments to Moodle forums
- Recording an instrument
- Recording the audio that is playing through your speakers
- Converting old K-7 recordings to digital audio

Combining music excerpts with voice comments can be interesting in our music course. In *Module 10 – What's good music?*, students will act as music critics and create a collaborative database of CD reviews. These reviews will consist of a short text accompanied by their own voice comments, interleaved with excerpts from the CD that they've chosen to review.

So let's have a look at how we can first capture our own voice, and later, remix it with music excerpts.

Selecting audio input

In the drop-down menu on Audacity's mixer toolbar, the first thing to choose is **Wave Out** or **Stereo Mix** as the input source. When we click on the **Record** button, Audacity will capture whatever sound is playing on our computer's speakers.

Tips for microphone capturing

For a better voice recording, most soundcards have an option to amplify the microphone signal. This option differs depending upon the operating system that we are using (Windows Vista, Windows XP, Linux), so the best thing to do is to perform a Web search with the keywords "mic + boost + operating system". We will be able to find guidance for your Operating System very easily. For Macs, usually the line-in doesn't have amplification, so the alternative is to buy an USB headset or a microphone amplifier.

Before we start recording, there's one last thing to keep in mind—the input volume. There is a potential problem that might arise from talking too close to the microphone—the sound can get distorted and the recording will be difficult to hear (we usually call this clipping or distortion). Another potential problem is the input being too low, and the recording will again be difficult to hear. The best way to control this is to use the Monitor input from Audacity, by going to the meter toolbar and clicking on this option from the input meter's pop-up menu, or just by clicking on the input meter (check Audacity's interface areas, discussed previously, if you have forgotten about it). If you have a microphone or other input source attached to your computer, you will be able to control the level of the audio before you start recording.

The input meter shows us many things—the left and right channels input level (the L and F bars), the average audio level (in a lighter red) and the peak audio level (in a darker red), and the peak hold lines at the right of the level bars show the maximum audio level achieved in the last three seconds:

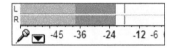

A good reference point when controlling the input volume in the mixer toolbar is the rightmost edge of the bar for the loudest audio level (and the average below that, of course). So we should try talking (especially in the parts we think will be louder), check the peaks, and control the input volume with the input volume slider in the meter bar:

Recording voice

Finally, we can click the Record button. Every time we press this button (after stopping the previous recording), a new track is created. If we are doing a retake because something went wrong in our first take, we can remove the previous track by clicking on the cross in the upper-left corner of the track, to close it.

Amplifying sound

If we still have an amplification problem, the solution is to amplify an audio selection. After selecting thee section of the recording that you want to amplify, go to **Effect | Amplify...** and increase the **Amplification (dB)**. Make sure that the wave form doesn't reach the top (value 1.0). For example, in the following screenshot, refer to the waveforms to the left of the first red bar and you can see a clipped recording. In the middle is a balanced recording, and on the right of the second red bar, is a recording with a low input level.

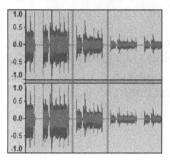

Importing audio tracks

We can import audio tracks to the project by going to the menu and clicking on **Project | Import Audio...** (or use the shortcut *Ctrl+I*). This can be useful for importing music tracks and alternating them with voice comments.

Moving tracks in the timeline

To re-order tracks in the timeline we can use the **Time shift** tool. By left-clicking on an audio track and dragging it to the left or right, we can position it where we want it in the timeline.

Reducing the MP3 file size of voice recordings

After we have all of the voice and music clips sequenced, we can export the result as an MP3 file. In the case of voice-only projects, and if it is not a special voice recording, we can save a lot of disk space, as follows. Before we start recording, we should go to the **Quality** tab in the **Audacity Preferences** and choose the **Default Sample Rate** as **11025 Hz**, **Default**, the **Sample Format** as **16-bit**, and in the **File formats** tab, select a **Bit Rate** of **48** kbps. Finally, export the project to MP3.

Remixing audio

Remixing audio is everywhere in the digital world. In TV and radio shows, Audio CDs, DVD movies—all of these use some degree of remixed audio from several sources.

We are now going to start mixing our music and sound effects, for the movie trailer soundtrack.

Cut, copy and paste

With the selection tool, we can cut, copy, and paste audio selections in the same way as in a text processor with regular text. But now, instead of paragraphs, the concept to use is a new audio track that is created to insert the copied or cut slices. We can then move these slices around, and sequence them as we saw previously with the Time shift tool.

Creating a new audio track

We can create an empty new audio track for our project. For this, we just need to go to **Project | New Audio Track**. Here we can cut and paste or copy and paste the selections in it.

Creating volume gradients using the Envelope tool

Editing the amplitude envelope lets us change the volume of a track, gradually over time, by adding a number of control points to the track. Each control point sets the amplitude (volume) at that point in time. This can be as low as zero, and as high as 150% of the normal maximum volume, and the volume is interpolated smoothly between the points.

The following screenshot shows a track for which an amplitude envelope was created, with the help of the Envelope Tool:

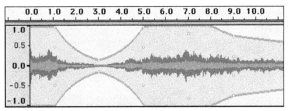

Source: members of the Audacity development team (2008). Envelope editing. Retrieved September 9, 2008, from http://audacity.sourceforge.net/onlinehelp-1.2/envelope.htm

In the preceding image, there are five control points at 1.0, 3.0, 5.0, 7.0, and 9.0 seconds. Each control point has up to four "handles", arranged vertically. The top and bottom handles are positioned at the target volume, and the middle handles are positioned a quarter-screen below, giving us a way to move the envelope above the 1.0 level.

To create a new control point, just click. To move a point, just drag. To remove a point, we have to click on it and drag it to an area outside of the track, and then release the mouse button.

Converting text to speech using Voki

Converting text to speech is a way that screen readers use to help visually impaired people to use the Web. It can also be used to add audio to forums, for example, if we don't have a microphone available, or we can even create avatars with different looks and different voices. We will use it in a roleplay game in a forum by using Voki in one of our course modules—*What's good music*—where students will have to create a character with its own voice that gives arguments to defend a music genre.

Voki (`http://www.voki.com`) allows us to create avatars that can talk either with our own voice or by converting text to speech.

The voices that are available in Voki are not perfect if we want to have something very formal, but it can be really fun for students (for example, matching a silly voice to a serious character).

To start using Voki, we have to create a new account and then, on the **Voki For My Site** tab, click on the **Create A New Voki** button:

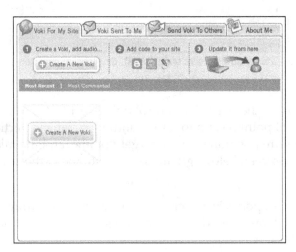

We can customize our character, select the gender, appearance, clothes, bling, background, and of course, give it a voice.

Giving voice to an avatar

After selecting an avatar's appearance, let's try giving it a voice by using text-to-speech (the second icon from the left). We have to type the text in the form, select the accent and voice alternatives and click on the the play button.

Note that we can also record directly from a phone, a microphone, or can upload an audio file.

After we have finished giving voice to our avatar, click on the **Done** button and then on the **Publish** button. A modal box will ask us to name the scene. Once we name it, the avatar is ready to be used. We can now embed it in Moodle by using the given code. If we use the code under **For Most Sites Use This Code**, we will again need to use the same HTML tags as for pasting it on a forum post and so on.

The result will be similar to the following:

Note that when embedding the Voki in Moodle, there will be a small advertisement below the avatar, for publicity.

Another tool worth mentioning is Gizmoz (`http://www.gizmoz.com`). This allows us to create an avatar from a photo, contrary to Voki.

Podcasting using Podomatic

A podcast can be thought of as a radio show that is distributed on the Web, just for subscribers. This means that when we, as authors, create a new "episode", our subscribers automatically receive it on their computer or an iPod (the Apple device that gave the name to this distribution mechanism) connected to the computer via a kind of synchronization process. Thus, a podcast is not the usual concept of radio, where a station is continually broadcasting. In addition, podcasts can be audio- or video-based (for example, `http://itunes.stanford.edu`). We also need a player to automatically download podcasts. We now have Songbird to compete with iTunes (Apple's media player). Songbird is a nice open source media player by Mozilla, the same guys who develop Firefox:

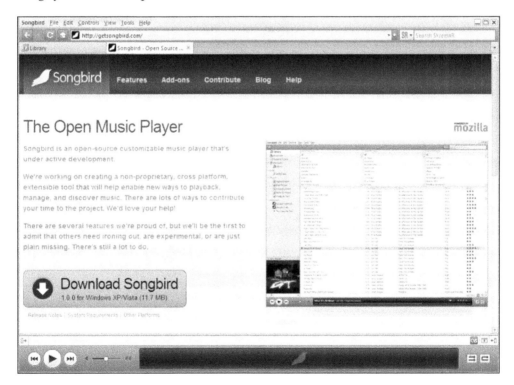

And with Podomatic, we are going to create podcasts, and we don't even need a player.

Podomatic (http://www.podomatic.com) is an online community that loves podcasting. We can create our own podcasts online, without the necessity to install any extra software. As an example of a podcast, we can create an audio magazine of what's going on in the course. We can talk about some of the activities that are being done, some things that we learned, and of course some songs that we've been listening to.

After creating a new account, we need to click on the **Post your first episode** button:

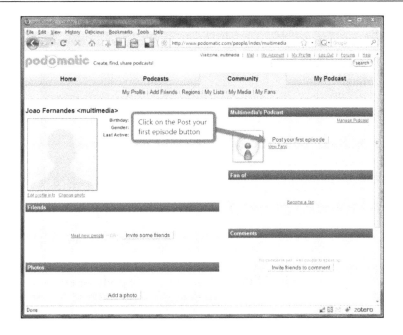

We can then upload files from our computer, or even record directly by using our webcam or microphone. Let's see, as an example, how to upload files. First, we should click on the **Upload media from your computer** link:

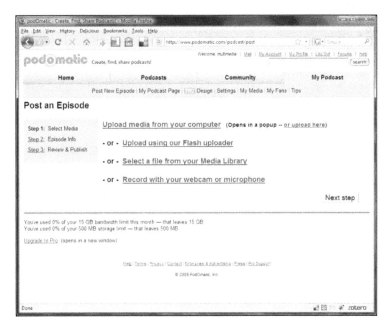

Next, click on the **Select some files** link and then select the required files from your computer:

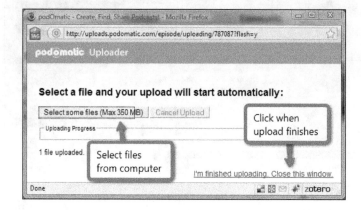

We have to specify any required information about the podcast episode, and then click on the **Next step** button when we are done:

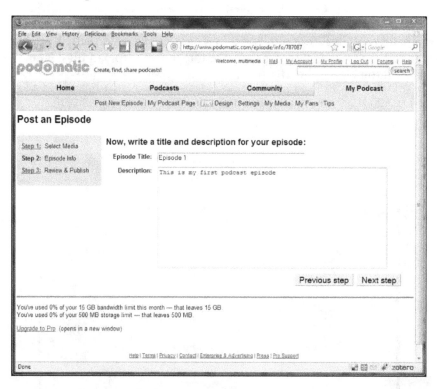

We can then upload a picture to go along with the episode, and add some tags to it, on the next screen after uploading the picture. In the example below, I added the Elephants Dream picture.

We can then review all of the information that we provided, and finally post the episode.

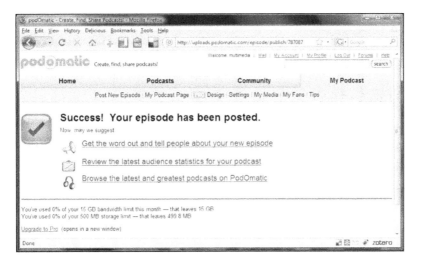

To add this podcast to Moodle, we need to click on the **Share Podcast** link, as shown in the following screenshot:

On the next screen, click on the **Embed a Player on Your Web Page** link.

Finally, we need to copy the embed code and paste it in Moodle. We can also add a link to the podcast on the course so that others can subscribe to it.

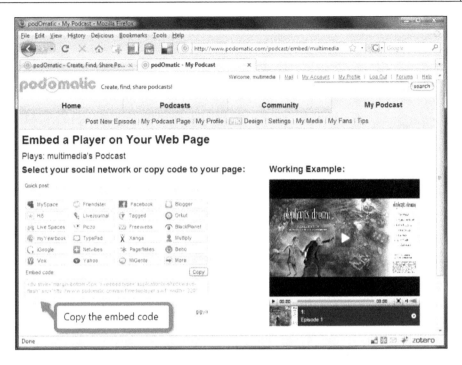

Summary

In this chapter, we focused on tasks for the Moodle integration of sound and music elements. The resources created will make information available in improved ways to students and will also get them engrossed in creating audio artifacts, such as slices, remixes, voice recordings, text-to-speech, and podcasts. We used several tools to achieve this, especially Audacity, VLC media player, Podomatic, and Imeem, and we also saw where to find free sounds and music.

Now that we can do some things with audio, why not try video? From stop-motion to video editing in general, to movies made out of photos, to online TV channels, it's all in the next chapter.

Video

This chapter will be dedicated to creating and editing videos for our course, from grabbing excerpts of video DVDs and making screencasts that record our screen actions, to proper video editing and stop motion animation. We will also learn how to download videos from online video sharing services and convert these to other formats.

By the end of this chapter you will be able to:

- Use a set of software tools for common procedures in video creation, editing, and broadcasting
- Publish and download videos from online video sharing services
- Convert a video format into several others and vice versa
- Create an online TV station
- Integrate video in Moodle

Finding free videos online

We should always keep in mind that we can use Wikimedia Commons and the Internet Archive (for example, `http://www.archive.org/details/moviesandfilms`) for downloading and using videos in our video projects. Although these are very useful, they are not the only services available; we can find many others, with particular interest to teachers and trainers. TeacherTube (`http://teachertube.com`) and YouTube (`http://www.youtube.com`) are the most well-known, and have lots of useful stuff.

But, before we see reference websites where we can find interesting videos and embed them in our courses, let's first have a look at the basics of video formats.

The basics of video formats

With video, things start to get complicated concerning formats. Rates, bitrates, codecs, formats, sizes, frame rates, and on top of this, all of the audio varieties, can overwhelm us. You should know some of these formats:

- **DV**: The format usually used by digital cameras for high quality video, corresponding to large file sizes.

- **AVI with XVid or DivX**: A common video format, using the XVid or DivX codecs, giving a good file size for movies converted from DVDs.

- **MPEG-2**: The DVD video format. If we explore a DVD file system, it contains VOB files, which are containers of video, audio, subtitles, and menus in this format.

- **MPEG-4**: A more recent format, for example, used by the iPhone. It can also be read by Flash player (not yet by the one in Moodle).

- **MOV**: Apple multimedia file format, similar to VOB, it also contains videos, along with other information such as subtitles.

- **WMV**: Windows Media Video, a format developed by Microsoft with a good quality-to-size ratio. It can be edited and exported easily in Windows operating systems, and uploaded to online video sharing services.

- **FLV**: Flash video, a more recent format used a lot in online video services such as YouTube. Has good file sizes for the Web and can be read by Flash player, which is present in most computers and browsers.

Remember that audio is a very important part of video and sometimes, when we use cheap cameras, we can have a good video and bad audio quality. We can solve this by either buying a proper digital camcorder or capturing the audio separately and mixing it with the video later on, with video editing software.

Webcams, mobile phones, and digital cameras use a certain video resolution (and also formats but that is another story) that reflect the size of the video in pixels (160x120, 320x240, 640x480, 720x576, and so on); so keep in mind that for screen playback, a size of 640x480 or above is the best. Whenever possible, choose this one, as it will also work well with online video services if you want to share it. Now let's see where to find some nice videos for our Moodle courses.

Instructables

On Instructables (http://www.instructables.com), we can find and share short videos about how to do things, from cooking to art, from how to make origami to robots.

Sclipo

Sclipo (`http://www.sclipo.com`) is a social learning network with a video library that can be used to support learning. To access it, we need to create a free account.

TrueTube

TrueTube (`http://www.truetube.co.uk`) is a place for debating social issues such as crime, environment, society, and so on. The main idea is to have young people discussing and posting their videos and views.

Academic earth

On the Academic earth website (`http://academicearth.org`), we can find many lectures from top scholars around the world.

Downloading YouTube and TeacherTube videos

Sometimes it can be useful to download videos from YouTube or other online video services if we want to show them at a time when we don't have an Internet connection, for example in a class.

Also, in some schools YouTube is blocked; so downloading videos is quite useful, despite the fact that at the time of writing this book, YouTube made an announcement that it is testing a Creative Commons licensing option and the possibility of downloading their hosted videos (see `http://www.youtube.com/blog?entry=Mp1pWVLh3_Y`, dated 12/02/2009). For now, there are some online tools that make this download, and even converting to other video formats, easy. With Movavi (`http://online.movavi.com`) we can download and convert videos from YouTube and several other video services on the Web, without installing any kind of software.

The interface is really easy to use, and we just need to follow these steps:

1. Enter the URL of the video (or upload a video if we click on **File**) in step 1, on the left-side of the page.

2. Select the video output format in step 2, at the center of the page.

3. Enter your e-mail address in step 3, on the right-side of the page.

4. Click on the **convert!** button.

The conversion can take a while, so an e-mail is sent when it is completed, providing a link that can be used to download the final video. Movavi can also process several videos at the same time (if we click on the plus (**+**) symbol in step 1 and add more URLs or files), merge videos in a single video (we have this option above the **convert!** button), and extract only the audio track of the video files (if we select MP3 or WMA as output format, again in step 2).

The available output formats are as follows:

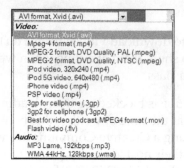

> Remember that if we download a video from YouTube as MPEG-2 we
> can edit it in Windows Movie Maker (a software that we will see later),
> but the originating file will be very large, taking a while to download. For
> example I downloaded a 3 minutes 37 seconds long video from Youtube,
> corresponding to a 116 MB file! That's why, if we just want to show a
> YouTube file in class, we should go for Flash video (FLV). YouTube uses
> this format (and MPEG-4 recently, because of the iPhone) and concerning
> our course, Moodle has a Flash player that can play this type of video out
> of the box (the multimedia filter should be active, though). This means
> that we only have to upload the Flash video to the course files area, and
> link to it using the HTML editor. A Flash player will be automatically
> inserted, and our students don't need any extra software to watch the
> video online. VLC Player, a tool we have seen in Chapter 2, can read
> Flash video, so if we want to play it on our PC (or project it during a class
> without sending it to Moodle), it can be very useful.

After we click on the **convert!** button, a progression bar and estimated time and size
will be shown. However, we cannot download the file immediately, so we need to
wait for the e-mail with the download link (the maximum time to wait can be 24
hours, but with small YouTube videos it's usually a matter of minutes). And if we
choose YouTube videos with a Flash video output, it takes less than a minute.

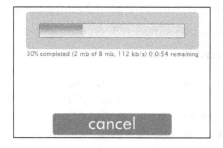

If we are in a hurry, and just need to get the video quickly, one option is to use Keepvid (`http://keepvid.com`). With this online tool we can directly download the video in MPEG-4 or FLV (Flash video) formats without the need for emails and waiting time. In this case, we just need to provide the URL and click on the **Download** button:

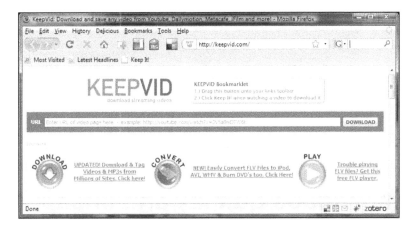

If we are using Mozilla Firefox, there's a very practical tool in Keepvid, called the **Bookmarklet**, that we can drag to the Firefox bookmarks toolbar, as seen in the following screenshot:

When we are watching a video and want to download it, we just need to click on this bookmark and the download links will be automatically created and presented to us, as seen in the following screenshot:

To download the video we just need to right-click on the download link and choose the **Save link as...** option.

With TeacherTube, we can directly download the videos in FLV format, using the download links that are provided:

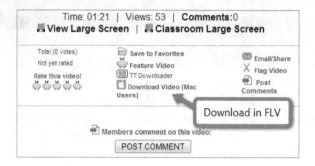

Creating videos quickly and cheaply

With so many digital cameras in the market, and the prices of storage going down, the tools to create and edit video are now more accessible to everyone. We will have a look at some techniques in the following sections, namely:

- Grabbing video selections from DVDs with VLC
- Editing video using Windows Movie Maker
- Creating photo stories (videos made of photos) with Windows Photo Story
- Creating screencasts (screen recordings) with Jing
- Creating an online TV with Mogulus
- Creating a stop motion movie with Animator DV Simple+

Let's begin by using the work of others in our creations, and extracting video selections from DVDs.

Grabbing video selections from DVDs

Extracting video selections from a DVD can be really useful, for example, if we want to edit a video that we have created with a digital camera that records onto DVD discs, or extract a selection from a regular DVD. In our course, in *Module 3 – Music and Media*, students are asked to create a movie trailer for the Elephant's Dream movie (as we saw earlier), so they will be required to extract several slices from the original DVD.

This is a Creative Commons licensed movie, so we don't have many copyright restrictions, but note that these instructions will still work with copyright protected DVDs (which includes most DVDs that you buy); also, be careful that you are not breaking any laws by doing so. Check Chapter 8 for further guidance on this.

After putting the DVD in the computer's DVD player, let's open VLC wizard again, as we saw with the CD ripping. Go to **File | Wizard...**, select the **Transcode/Save to file** option, and click on the **Next** button.

In the next window, we will have to define the input again, as we did for the Audio CD. After clicking on the **Choose** button, select the **Disc** tab (refer to the following screenshot), select **DVD** under **Disc type**, insert the **Title** number (and chapter, subtitles, and audio track if the DVD has more and if you want other than the standard ones), and click on the **OK** button.

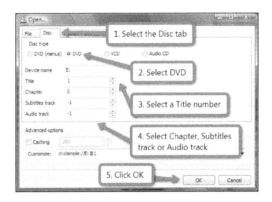

DVD movies are organized according to **Titles**, which are the main video files (**Title 1** is usually the main movie and **Title 2** could be, for example, some extra material—most of the time, there is no need to change the subtitles or audio tracks values), and these titles are made out of chapters. The best thing to do is to open the disc in VLC (**File | Open Disc... | DVD**) and try the title numbers before performing the transcoding, to see if VLC plays the title that we intend to rip.

Going back to the **Input** window (refer to the following screenshot), we have the possibility of just making a **Partial Extract**, copying to our computer, for example, just one minute of a movie. If we enable this option (in this movie, it won't be needed), we will have to define the start and end time of the selection, in seconds. This could be repeated several times and it would save us time and disk space because instead of ripping an entire DVD, we would just extract the important parts. To get the value of the time period in seconds, while playing the DVD in VLC, we have to identify the time intervals (in minutes and seconds), convert it to seconds (by multiplying by 3600 the hours value, adding the minutes value times 60, and adding the value in seconds. Here's an example:

Values in seconds for the time period between 01:30:15 and 01:40:30 are:

- 01:30:15 = (01 hours x 3600 seconds) + (30 minutes x 60 seconds) +
  (15 seconds) = 3600 + 1800 + 15 = 5415 seconds

- 01:40:30 = (01 hours x 3600 seconds) + (40 minutes x 60 seconds) +
  (30 seconds) = 3600 + 2400 + 30 = 6030 seconds

In the next example, we would capture just the second minute of the movie, between 60 (1 minute = 1x60s) and 120 (2 minutes = 2x60s) seconds:

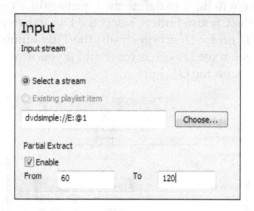

After we click on **Next**, we will go the **Transcode** window. DO NOT choose either of the options shown, that is, transcode video or audio, just click on the **Next** button again. In the next window, **Encapsulation format**, select **MPEG 1**, and then click on **Next**.

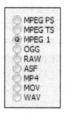

Finally, we just have to select the location in which to save the file, and define the file suffix as **.avi**:

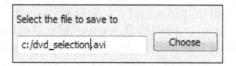

After we click on the **Finish** button, VLC will start converting the file, and we will see this in the status bar at the bottom of the main application window. The time will advance as the process continues, and depending on our CPU, it can be faster or slower. Either way, as we are not transcoding (converting it to another video format), the process will be a quick one (probably less than 15 minutes for the entire Elephant's Dream movie).

The resulting files in this kind of process can be quite large. This is because we are not using any encoding of the original file (remember VOB files that make up a DVD are MPEG-2 encoded), making the process faster, but demanding more in terms of the amount of disk space required. Each minute of video will need around 50 MB of disk space, meaning that the 10 minute movie we are extracting will need approximately 500 MB! We are using this process because it is the best way to work with the video in a video editing software application, in this case Windows Movie Maker 2 (something we will see right away). Later on, after editing it in this tool, we will transcode the final video to the WMV codec, which can save some space.

Editing videos using Windows Movie Maker

Editing video nowadays has become as easy as editing text. In contrast to the time when we had to use scissors or Video Cassette Recorders and lots of cables, we can now film and edit raw videos with a cheap camera or mobile phone and a few clicks, with great contributions to the education field, for example:

- To debate scenes from a film.
- To publish a study trip video.
- Create an end of year school presentation with several video clips from the school year.
- Create simple documentaries (in science or social sciences, for example about a national or regional nature park, a school, a community issue, and so on).
- Organize a contest of student-made videos of practical activities (science experiments, artistic performances, and so on).

- Create video tutorials about playing a musical instrument or, for example, to teach a gestural language.
- Create video "papers", for example, in a teacher training context, where a trainee is filmed during a class and then creates a web document where he embeds video clips and text about several key events and reflects on them. This can also apply to comments on presentations or daily events in general.

We will now see how we can do this kind of video using Windows Movie Maker, starting first by creating a two-and-a-half minutes trailer of the movie Elephant's Dream that we have ripped previously, and adding a new soundtrack to it.

Windows Movie Maker is an easy-to-use, free video editing software that comes with Microsoft Windows XP and Vista. The interface is really simple, with the following five main areas:

- The **Top menu**, with the well-known **File** menu, the **Import Media** button, undo, redo, and other functions
- The **Tasks** sidebar, that can show the multimedia collections in Movie Maker
- The **Central Panel**, where we can access the project files, and the different effects and transitions
- The **Previewing monitor**, where we can watch previews of the clips, effects, transitions, and the entire edited movie
- The **Storyboard/Timeline**, where we can sequence our movie and add effects, transitions, titles, and control extra audio tracks — but only one in addition to the original audio from the video clips

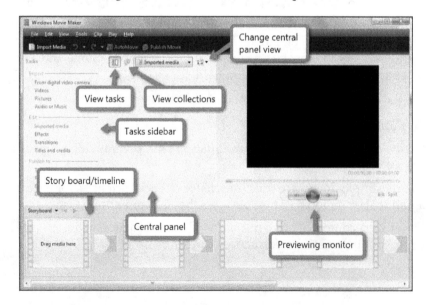

The advantage of this kind of software (and its equivalent in Apple, iMovie) is that it usually comes with the operating systems of the computers in schools, so it's easy to start working. I've chosen this software, and not iMovie, because Windows Movie Maker is more widely-spread and because, unfortunately, there is no free software that can match it (in terms of interface, functionality, and simplicity). There was Avid free DV (http://www.avid.com/freedv) until some time ago, but it was discontinued; so we will have to stick to the Microsoft solution. Some of the processes are common in iMovie and in other video editing software, so it is hoped that they will also be helpful for Mac users.

I have used Movie Maker with students to make the first video story board of a class documentary about the Sado nature reserve in Portugal. I divided the class into groups, each of them with a theme (dolphins, geology, flora, insects, conservation, and so on) and they had to research and create a story, deciding which places to film, and prepare a written argument that would later support the chosen voice-off to narrate the story (we voted for the best voice, after some auditions). We then made a study trip and filmed some elements (most of the filming was made by myself and two students, although not on this study trip). After we had the video (some hours in DV format, we split it into several files, still using a lot of disk space), we had a computer room for some weeks to make the first drafts from the raw film, using Movie Maker, which were joined and later edited in Adobe Premiere, which is more flexible than Movie Maker. The final result can be seen at http://www.youtube.com/watch?v=QjXSuOP5y7o.

Because the computer room where they initially worked was not always available, I managed to get a shared faster computer in a room where they could go when the class wasn't in session, and schedule its use on a sheet on the wall next to it. Video editing takes time, so this is something to keep in mind. The disk space is a very important issue too. Avoiding duplicating video files is fundamental. In this kind of collaborative work, all of the editing work should be done in Movie Maker on the same set of files. When they edit a movie in Movie Maker based on these sources, it doesn't mean that they are actually splitting, merging, and deleting the original files, but just marking locations in a project file. This is very useful if we want to work on several computers, because we just need to keep the common set of files in a shared folder, and when they open their project, Movie Maker asks for the location of the source files. In this way, it's easy to move between computers (we just need to transfer the Movie Maker project) and avoid duplication. So let's start by creating this project file.

Creating a project

After we open Movie Maker, the first thing that we need to do is create a project. Just like in Audacity, this application organizes several elements (videos, sound files, images, titles, and transitions) in one file, the so-called **Windows Movie Maker Projects** file, with the `.MSWMM` extension. So we can first create a folder in our PC, with the following subfolders: `audio`, `video`, `images` and then, in Movie Maker, go to **File | Save Project As...**, in the previously-created folder and save the project (with a name of your choice, just make sure that you don't use spaces or uppercase, just plain text with underscores replacing the spaces — this is a good practice if we want to share these files in Moodle later). The best practice in video editing (and editing in general) is to have all of the files for the project in a single folder, as it makes it easier to not lose our sources when we backup our data, and makes it easy to transfer the project and all of its files to another workstation. Here's an example of what my trailer project folder looks like:

Creating a collection

Movie Maker allows us to have hundreds of files in the central panel area. With time, and if we use it a lot in several projects, this area will have all of the elements that we imported in previous projects. One of the ways of avoiding huge lists of media elements is to organize them in collections (and sub-collections, if it's a really complicated project), one for each project. This means that we will import all of the multimedia elements for this project into a virtual folder in Movie Maker. To create this collection, we first have to change the sidebar view to **Collections**. We can do this by clicking on the **View | Collections** button. The sidebar will now be named **Collections**, and we can add a new collection by right-clicking on it, selecting **New Collection Folder**, and naming it with the name of the project:

We can repeat this process to create new collections or sub-collections. We can also duplicate collections by copying and pasting, removing, or renaming them. These collections do not represent the physical folders on our hard disk, but virtual folders in Movie Maker, so we will not actually be duplicating files if we duplicate collections.

Importing multimedia (starting with video)

We will now import the main video file that we have extracted from the DVD into the Movie Maker project. After moving the original **.avi** file that we extracted with VLC to the video sub-folder of the project, we have to click on the **Import media** button and select it. But before that, we should make sure that the new collection folder that we have created in the sidebar is selected. In this way, the imported video file will be included in it. After this, we can change the view of the central panel to **Details**, as shown in the following screenshot:

This can show us a lot more elements in the same window than the thumbnails mode.

Splitting

Just like in Audacity, we can use the *Spacebar* key to start and stop the playback of the movie file in the previewing monitor area. This is very practical, because we can find the right moment where we want to split the video and just press the *Spacebar* key instead of using the mouse and clicking on the pause button. We can also fine-tune our splitting frame, by using either the buttons in the monitoring window or the *J* and *L* keys, for the previous and next frames respectively.

To split the video clip, after selecting the exact moment of splitting, we have to click on the **Split** button, or press the *M* key. We will get another clip in the central pane with the name of the original video followed by a **(1)**. Suppose we want to use a clip for the trailer that is between **01:20** and **2:39** of the original video (the running of the characters in a moving path, in the case of Elephants Dream). In this case, we will have to to use the split function twice, having the following result:

- original_video_name: Made of the first 1:20 of the original video
- original_video_name (1): The selection we wanted, lasting 1:19
- original_video_name (2): The rest of the original video after 2:39

A useful thing to do, every time we obtain a video selection to use in our final movie, is to rename it, giving it the name of its main characteristic. This can help in the next phase of adding the clips to the story board in Movie Maker. To do this, we have to right-click on the clip and then click on the **Rename** option. In this case, I have renamed the originating clip to **long run**:

elephants_dream	00:01:20	00:00:00	00:01:20
long run	00:01:19	00:01:20	00:02:39
elephants_dream (2)	00:07:56	00:02:39	00:10:35

We can do this several times and, in the end, delete all of the unwanted clips from our collection. If we want to repeat parts of a clip that we already have, the best thing to do is to import the original movie again and create new clips, eliminating the "trash".

Creating a story board

When we have all of the clips required to make the final trailer, it's time to sequence them on the storyboard. This is really easy, as it works by drag and drop. We just have to drag one clip at a time to the storyboard, in the required order of appearance.

long run

Inserting transitions and effects

Inserting transitions and effects is as easy as moving the clips to the story board. If we click on **Transitions** in the Collections side bar, we get thumbnails of the several options that are available to us in the central panel. If we click on each of them, we can preview it in the monitor, by clicking on the the Play button or by pressing the *Spacebar* key. The same applies to **Effects**:

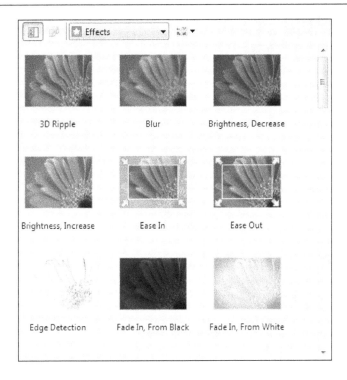

We can try some of the transitions and effects, specially the **Cross Dissolve**, **Fade Out, To Black**, and **Fade In, From Black**. To apply an effect to a clip in the story board, we should drag it from the central panel to the bottom left corner of the clip. To apply a transition, we should drag it from the central panel to the rectangle between clips in the storyboard. Visually, we will get something similar to the following screenshot:

To remove a transition, we just need to select it and press the *Delete* key. To remove effects we can use the same procedure, but because we can add several effects to the same clip, if we right-click on the star in the lower-left corner of a clip in the storyboard, and then click on **Effects**, we can remove specific effects, as these will be listed here.

Inserting a title at the beginning of the movie

To add a title at the beginning of the movie, go to the top menu and select **Tools | Titles and Credits...** and then, click on **Title at the beginning**. The same applies for titles before the selected clip, title overlays, and credits at the end of the movie.

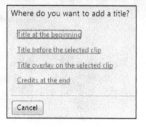

Inserting an image at the end of the movie

Movie Maker also allows us to insert images, which will be displayed for a certain amount of time into the storyboard. Before importing the image by using the **Import media** button, we can define the amount of time for which the image will be displayed, by going to **Tools | Options | Advanced** and changing the values for the **Picture duration**. We can also change the video properties, such as the **Aspect ratio**, but we will keep the 4:3 ratio, because the idea in the end is to upload the video to YouTube or TeacherTube.

There are a couple of things to keep in mind when we add images to a movie. One of them would be the size of the picture in pixels. Its size should be at least the same as that of the video (in this video, with an original size of 720x576 pixels, the image should have the same size or, if larger, should have the same proportion). This will avoid distortions and loss of quality in the final movie. We can also add effects to the images.

Removing the original soundtrack and inserting a new one

Despite the fact that Movie Maker has a narration option, the best thing to do is to capture voice and remix it with the rest of the music and sound effects in Audacity, and then import it to Movie Maker and define it as the movie soundtrack. One of the reasons for this is that Movie Maker only allows one audio track; so if we wanted to add voice with background music that would be a problem. Another reason is that you cannot control the quality of the voice recording and mixing in Movie Maker as you can in Audacity.

To add a new soundtrack that will replace the clips' soundtrack, go to **Tools | Audio Levels...** and move the slider to the limit on the right, that is, **Audio/Music**.

After this step, and after importing the complete soundtrack to one of our Collections (in MP3 format), we have to change the storyboard view to timeline mode. For that, in the top left corner of the storyboard, click on the **Storyboard** button and select the **Timeline** option.

In the timeline, we can drag the soundtrack file to the **Audio/Music** track, and it's done.

Publishing the edited movie

To get the best quality possible, the export format for the completed trailer should be AVI. But we already saw that this format is space-consuming, and as we want to send the video to YouTube or TeacherTube, the WMV format, that is, Windows Media Video, would be preferred. On the **File** menu, click on **Publish Movie...**, select the **This computer** option, name your movie, and finally, in the **More settings** tab, select the **Windows Media VHS Quality (PAL)(1.0 Mbps)** option. Click on **Publish** once you are done:

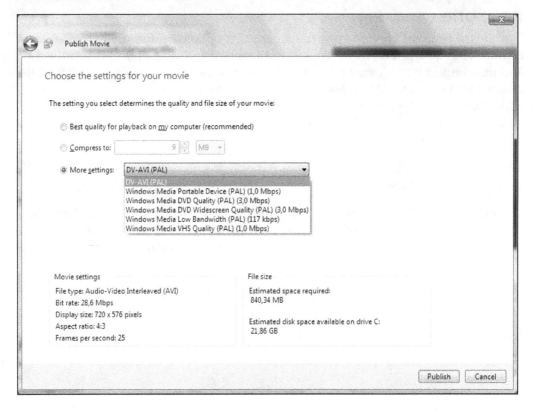

The video will start converting, and we are then ready to use it in Moodle.

Moodle it!

We have two ways of adding a video to Moodle. The first is to send the video files to the course files area, later linking to it. The other is to upload the video to an online video service and later embed it in Moodle.

Uploading video directly to Moodle

Moodle, as we saw, has several multimedia plug-ins that automatically recognize a link to a multimedia file, such as a video, and automatically embed a player. If we upload the video in WMV format to our course, Windows Media Player will play it in the browser window. However, when we talk about the Web we are looking for cross-platform compatibility, and WMV can be a problem for Mac and Linux users, at least with embedded players. One of the solutions to this problem is to convert the video into the FLV format by using Movavi online, as we saw previously. The other is to upload our video to an online video service, such as YouTube or TeacherTube.

Uploading videos to TeacherTube (or YouTube)

Uploading our videos (including our students' videos) to a service such as TeacherTube has several advantages:

- If we don't have much space on our Moodle server, this will not load it with more files, particularly a video that is usually associated with large file sizes

- If we have many students trying to watch the same video in Moodle's files area, this will affect the server performance

- As it uses the Flash video format, problems of different formats, players, and operating systems are solved

- If we publish it on these online services, other people can see and comment on it (this can be an advantage or not, depending on what we want however, we can make some videos private)

We will now see how to send the published video to TeacherTube (in YouTube the process will be quite the same, with some changes in forms).

After we create an account in TeacherTube, we are taken to our account page:

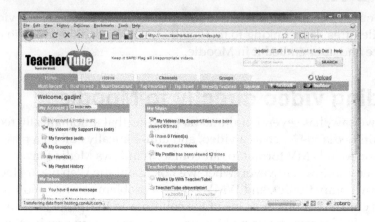

After we click on the **Upload** link, we need to fill in some forms about the video that we want to upload:

The next step is to upload the file and select whether we want the video to be public or private (the second option can be useful if we are concerned about e-safety — check Chapter 8 for this):

After we click on the **Upload button**, it's done. It will take some time until the video is ready but then, as we saw in Chapter 1, we will just need to use the embed code associated with the video to add it to Moodle, and show our trailer to everyone.

Creating a photo story with Windows Photo Story

Stories made out of photos are a good way to describe an event, make a presentation, or create a storyboard for a movie made out of scenes. In our course, in *Module 5 – Being a musician*, every student will have to build a presentation of his or her favorite artist, based on some photos of their performances, albums, and so on. I will use as an example Antônio Carlos Jobim, the great Brazilian bossa nova composer who left a great part of his work available to the public, after his death, at http://www.jobim.org.

Photo Story 3 for Windows is a very simple software application that can be used to create videos out of photos by combining audio, text, effects, and transitions. Simpler than Movie Maker, it can be used by younger students as it provides a step-by-step interface that guides the user through to the final publishing of the video. In case it is not installed on the school's computers, we will need to ask one of the administrators to download and install it from http://www.microsoft.com/windowsxp/using/digitalphotography/PhotoStory/default.mspx.

After opening Photo story 3, we are presented with the following window:

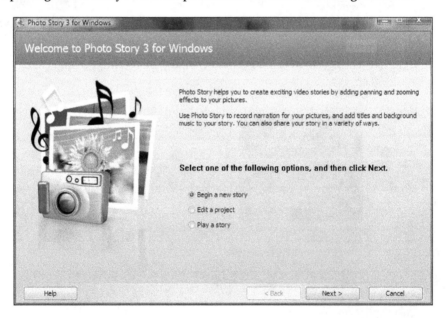

A good way to start a Photo Story project is to create a folder for the project and subfolders for the photos (for example, based on the periods of the life of the artist and/or types of images that we have gathered, such as CD covers, photos, or screenshots). Remember that the photos should have approximately the same quality and at least a minimum size in pixels according to the desired photo story size (640x480 or larger is good if we are planning to publish the photo story with this size or less). After obtaining these and saving them in the correct folders, it's time to open Photo Story 3, select **Begin a new story** and click on **Next**. We are taken to the first step of our photo story creation process:

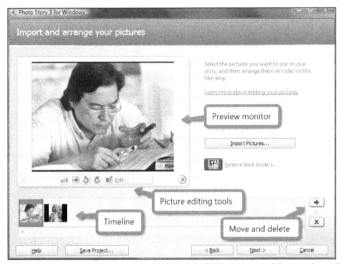

Source: Instituto Antonio Carlos Jobim (2008). P64f002. Retrieved September 12, 2008, from `http://www.jobim.org/jspui/`

Importing pictures

Now we should click on the **Import Pictures...** button and select the pictures that we want to add. These will be added to the timeline, and we can edit them by using the available tools (these tools, from left to right, are **Correct Color levels**, **Correct Red Eye**, **Rotate Counter clockwise**, **Rotate Clockwise**, **Edit**). After we select a picture for editing in the timeline (it gets a blue frame around it), let's save the project by clicking on the **Save Project...** button and saving it to the previously created folder in WP3 format.

Now let's take a look at the **Edit Pictures** option:

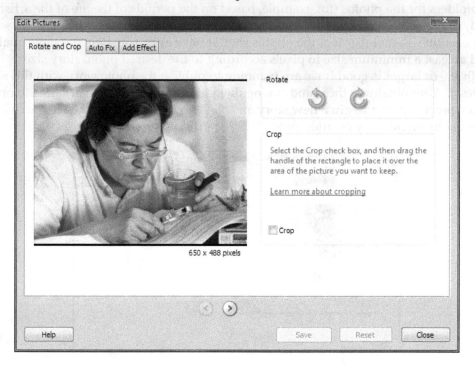

The first tab, **Rotate** and **Crop**, has options to rotate and crop the picture. Once we select the image for editing, we can crop the picture automatically, removing the black areas around it (for example, if it has a portrait orientation), by clicking on the **Remove black borders...** link in the previous screenshot. If we want to roll back our changes, there is a **Reset** button in the lower-right corner. We can also make some corrections via the **Auto fix** and **Add Effects** tabs, such as:

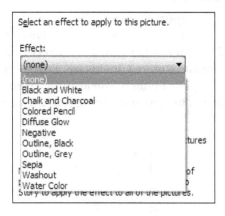

After editing the pictures and clicking on the **Save** and **Close** buttons (if we click only on the **Close** button, our changes will be lost) we can reorder the pictures in the timeline either by dragging and dropping or by using the arrows to the right of the timeline. To delete a picture, we just need to select it, and then press the *Delete* key or click the button with the cross at the right of the timeline. We can also use the **Import pictures** button as many times as we wish, adding more pictures to the project. Moreover, we should make sure that we save the project once in a while, to avoid losing any of our pictures.

Adding titles to pictures

After we click **Next** on the previous screen, it's time to start adding titles to the pictures. To the right of the image we have a form that can be used to add text, and some formatting tools above it. Note that we can also add effects to the picture at this phase, by using the button below the preview monitor.

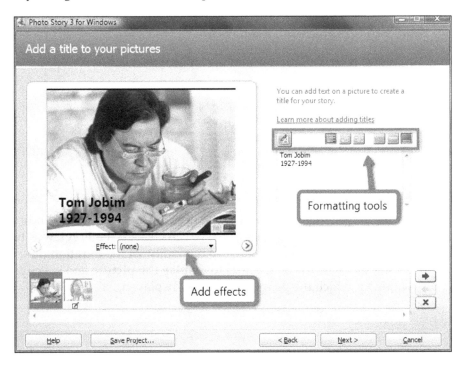

The formatting icon on the left allows us to select fonts, font sizes, and colors.

Adding narration and motion

After we click on **Next**, we can now add narration and add motion to our pictures. If we are doing something simple, this is a quick way of doing it. An alternative is to create the narration (mixed with or without music) in Audacity and add it as soundtrack on the next screen.

A nice way of adding dynamism to our static pictures is to create a zoom in/out of a particular detail of the picture. For this, we can click on **Customize Motion...**.

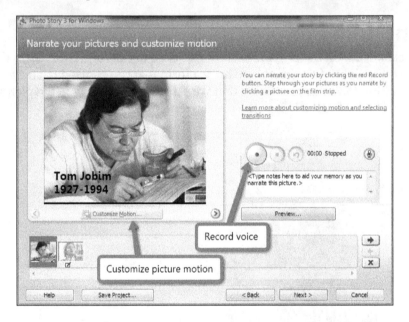

Now we can resize the picture area that we want to show as starting and ending points, and Photo Story will do the transition. We can click on the **Preview...** button to see a preview of the final result. We can also manually set the duration time of the picture by selecting the **Number of seconds to display the picture** and specifying the number of seconds for which the picture should be displayed.

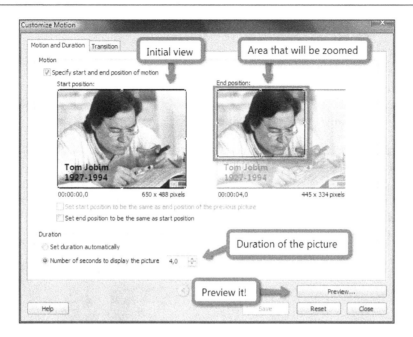

If we select the **Transition** tab, we can add some transitions between pictures. Again, we can have a look at the result by clicking on the **Preview...** button.

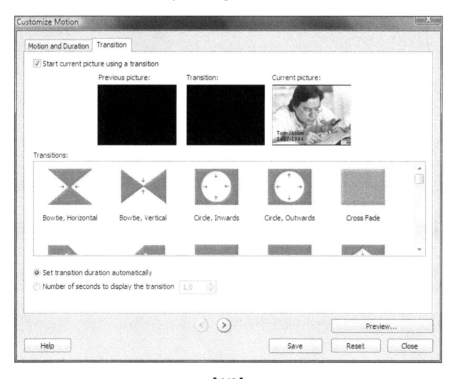

Adding background music

After clicking on the **Next >** button again, we can add a background audio track. We should make sure that before clicking on the **Select music...** button, we have selected the photo where the audio track should begin (with a blue frame around it). This is usually the first one (we can also use several soundtracks for each photo, but with less control when compared to using an audio editing software).

The volume slider, in case we used the narration tool previously, is a way of balancing both voice and music added in this step. As I had mentioned, using Audacity will increase the possibilities, so an alternative way of adding audio to the photo story is to publish it without any voice or music and then, in Movie Maker, combine the audio created with Audacity (with multi-track, more control of the recording process, synchronization, and so on) and eventually combine it with other videos.

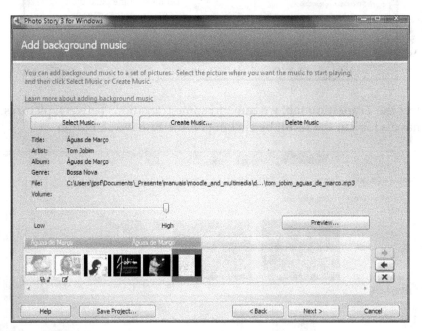

Publishing the Photo Story

Finally, it's time to publish the Photo Story. After you click on **Next >**, you will be presented with a few options for saving the movie (in WMV format). The first step is to select the destination of the file, usually computer playback, followed by the location to which the final result should be saved. We can then refine the quality settings by clicking on the **Settings** button:

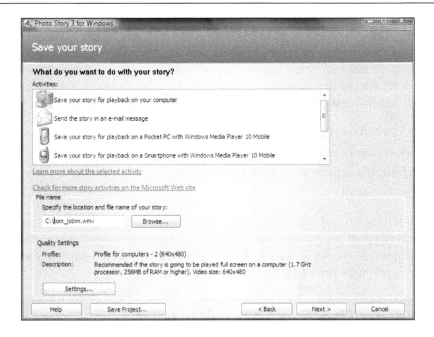

A good setting for computer playback and for uploading the resulting video to TeacherTube is **Profile for computers – 2 (640x480)**. This will give us a good file size without great quality losses in full-screen. And now, we just have to click on the **OK** button followed by the **Next >** button, and the Photo Story will become a video!

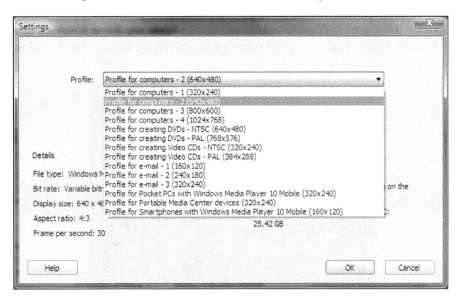

We can then upload it to TeacherTube, as we have seen previously.

Creating a screencast with Jing

Screencasts are recordings of screen actions, and are very useful for showing procedures in a computer interface, as they reveal the mouse movements, clicking, typing, and more than that, audio comments. With Jing, it's really easy to create screencasts, just like the commented screenshots we saw previously. We just have to:

1. Select a screen region.
2. Click on the record button.
3. Perform the actions with audio comments.
4. Save the result.

Screencasts will be an important part of our course, as we will use them to create tutorials that support students in the use of the several tools used in the course activities. Jing saves the screencast in Flash format (SWF) which we will then make available as a resource (link to a file) in our course.

Recording the screen with audio

Just before starting the screencast, we need to connect the microphone and headphones (the headset) to the audio ports in our computer, with the pink jack to the pink connector and the green jack to the green connector respectively.

After preparing the screen region or application window, we have to click on the "Sun" and then on the **Capture** button, selecting the area to record. Now, instead of clicking on the **Capture Image** button, we need to click on the **Capture Video** button. A countdown warning of the microphone being on is displayed, and then the recording starts.

When the screencast is completed, after clicking on the **Stop** button, we can preview the recording and choose where we want to save it. Let's click on the **Save** button and select the destination folder, to save the video in SWF format.

To add our screencasts to Moodle

We can upload our recording to YouTube (or Screencast, another service associated with Jing) but we can also upload it to Moodle if we need to. As we will be uploading a SWF file, there is a multimedia filter in Moodle that will automatically embed the video. But the problem is that Moodle's SWF plugin has a standard size of 400x300 px (that can be changed in the `filter/mediaplugin/filter.php` file in any Moodle installation), and if we create a screencast without these dimensions, it will get deformed. Luckily, there is a trick to change it to the size of our screencast. For this, using the HTML editor, we should click on the **Link** button and then on the **Browse** button and upload the screencast file to Moodle's files area. After clicking on the name of the uploaded file, we get the link in the URL form. We just have to add the following code to the end of that URL:

`?d=widthx(height+25)`

These extra 25 pixels to the height of the Flash player are related to the player controls and should always be added when including Jing screencasts. In a movie with 640x480 we would insert the following code:

`?d=640x505`

Remember to register the size of the screencast in Jing, and add, for example, a reference to it in the file name.

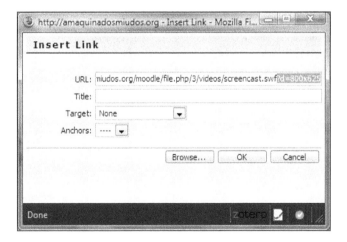

Creating an online TV station using Mogulus

Who would have guessed that we would live a time when anyone can make his or her own TV station with a computer, an Internet connection, and a cheap camera? And you can ignore the camera if you wish. With so many videos on the Web, it's really simple to get raw material for your programming. Imagine a TV in our Moodle course with several programs, with live news directly from a webcam, videos made by you, or by others that are part of this programming, and you will have an idea of what am I talking about. And you can set it all up in 15 minutes. Yes, 15 minutes!

I can imagine 100 ways we that we could use this in a school, and in Moodle in particular, to broadcast:

- A live school event, such as a school play
- Old school events (such as a history of our school)
- Classes (theatre, games in physical education classes, science experiments, and so on)
- Shows made by students and teachers
- Meetings, workshops, and clubs activities
- Online videos selected by teachers or students, something similar to a pick of the day
- And many more

In our course, students will be required to create a course channel that will be available in a sideblock. They will be using Mogulus, and design all of it in a collective way. They will start by building a foundation document for the station, with editorial standards and policies, the main theme, the programs and the teams responsibilities, using a wiki to develop each of these aspects. And they will use Mogulus for all of this.

Mogulus (http://www.mogulus.com) is an online service that broadcasts TV stations made by its users and makes available a complete online TV production studio for this purpose. On the front page, we can access many channels that are broadcasting live.

To start using this tool, we need to sign up and select a name for our channel.

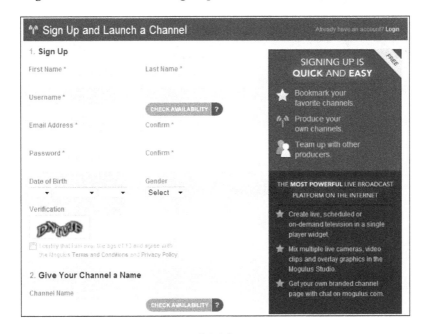

If we follow all of the given steps, we will be taken to the **Configure Your Channel Page**, where we can add a description of the channel, and specify some other settings:

After we are done with this, staying in the **Configure Channel** tab, we can define the channel style, and select for example, a corner bug (the logo of the channel that is always at the corner of the screen of regular TVs):

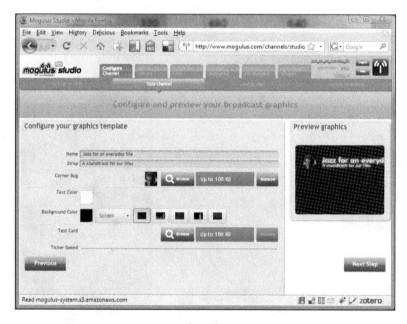

We also have other options in the **Manage Team** and **Advertising** sections, which allow us to add more collaborators to the channel programming effort, and insert advertising if we want to earn some money with the channel. As of now, we will just worry about our library so that we can start broadcasting our channel. When we click on the **Manage Library** tab, we can search or upload videos.

There are two important things to keep in mind in this area:

- The **Your first storyboard** section will contain a sequence of videos that will be broadcast. We can add new storyboards and folders to organize the videos. We just have to drag them inside a newly-created folder. To change the names of the folders and storyboards, we can double-click on the names, and edit these as per requirement.

- The options for importing the video from the Web are under the pink toolbar. By default, we can search for videos on YouTube, but we can also upload videos from our computer.

We will try the easiest method, that is, using ready-made videos from YouTube by using the **Enter your video search query here** search form that you can see in the previous screenshot. The search results are displayed on the rightmost part of the window:

We can now add the movies to the storyboard by dragging and dropping them from one place to the other.

If everything works fine, then when we click on **Your first storyboard**, we will find a sequence of videos (some of them will be in the conversion process by Mogulus) and a test video that we can delete (by clicking on the cross on the right-hand side of the video). Finally, we can proceed to the **Broadcast Live** tab:

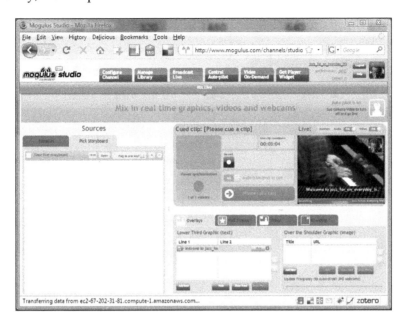

By default, we will be asked if the Flash player can access any webcam that we have connected. We can select sources for the broadcast—either camera or storyboards. We can also control overlays or tickers (the extra-information that scrolls along the screen, that we usually see on the news channels) for messages that we want to show along with the videos:

If we wanted to add a moment of webcam between videos, we can cue it and then make a transition, mixing it live. But first, if we want to program the channel so that it keeps on playing a selection of videos (and different storyboards), we need to go to the **Control Auto-pilot** tab:

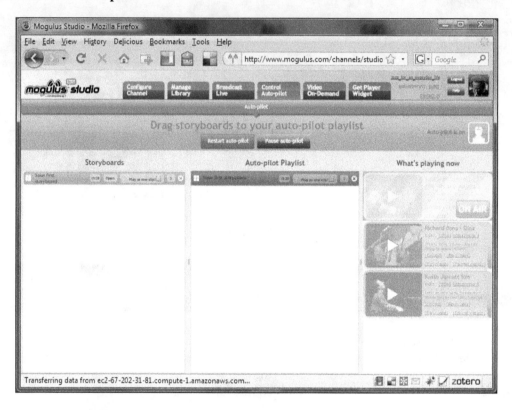

In this phase, we just need to drag the sequences of videos that we want Mogulus to keep in a loop as a live broadcast of our channel, from the **Storyboards** column to the **Auto-pilot Playlist** column.

We can also activate the **Video On-Demand** option by going to this tab, meaning that any viewer can search for videos and storyboards that we have broadcasted.

Finally, we can obtain the embed code for the TV player that we can paste into Moodle:

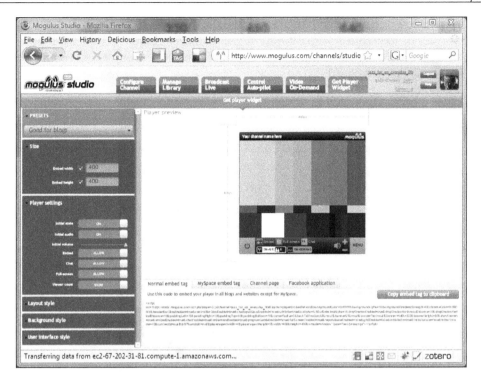

And in our course side block, we will have our channel:

Creating a stop motion movie with Animator DV Simple+

When I was a kid I had a flipbook that when flipped, showed a woman getting up from bed. Page by page, the changes were too small to notice but from beginning to end, they meant the difference between being in bed and being up. In stop motion, this is the main concept—the accumulation of small changes of position in usually non-moving objects that, when properly sequenced, simulate movement.

For the course in our module dedicated to music, dance and emotions, one of the tasks will be to create a stop motion movie of a clay character that will be breakdancing. For this we will use Animator DV Simple + (`http://animatordv.com/download7`). Download it from `http://www.download.com` and use the provided serial number.

To start, we should:

1. Connect our camcorder or webcam to the computer and then open Animator DV Simple +.

2. Create a new folder by clicking on the **New Folder** button.

3. Create a **New Project**, and then click on the **OK** button.

4. In the **Settings** dialog box, select the capture device that we will be using, by clicking on the **Set** button and then **OK**. We can leave the rate of 15 frames per second as the default. This means that we will need to capture 15 frames for each second of film!

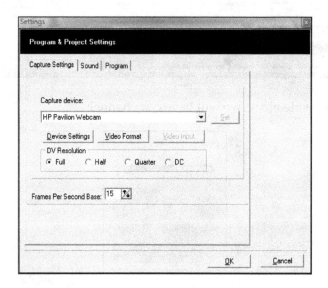

The standard interface will appear, as shown in the following screenshot:

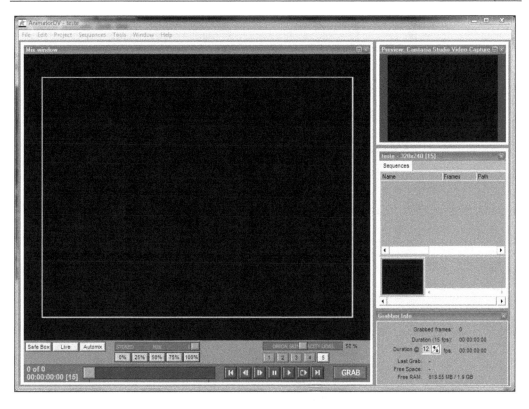

5. Click on the **GRAB** button (or press the *Spacebar*— this is the keyboard shortcut) to capture the first frame.

6. We are asked to create a new sequence, and name it, as seen in the following screenshots.

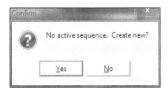

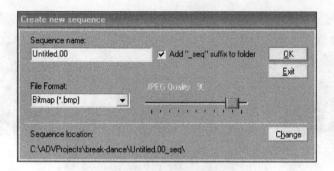

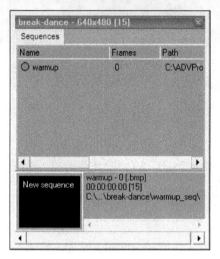

7. Click on the **GRAB** button, move the clay man a little bit and grab another frame, repeating the process until we have a major sequence completed. We can control the grabbing of new frames with the onion skin functionality. This allows us to see the previous position of the object with a level of opacity a little bit below the next image to be captured by the camera, similar to a "ghost" of the previous frame.

> Onion skin functionality is a base for creating animations. In addition, you can also fix the direction and speed of recorded objects. The onion skin function unites several frames of a sequence, giving them transparency (an onion skin opacity level) in relation to each other. The result is one picture with several former frames. The number of these frames is defined by the present "Onion Skin Level" parameter, on a scale of 1-99.

8. Use the *CTRL+L* key to preview the sequence of frames, in video format.

We can use the *Delete* key to delete any frame that wasn't captured at the required level of quality. In the **Sequences** dialog box, we can right-click on the sequence that is being recorded to deactivate it and then start a new sequence. This can also be used to export the sequence to AVI, and later worked on in Windows Movie Maker or in any other video editing software application.

Finally, to upload the movie to Moodle, we could, for example, publish the final video to YouTube and embed it or convert the movie to WMV and make it available in the course page as a file, as we saw previously.

Summary

In this chapter, we focused on video production and editing, looking at different ways of using these in Moodle. We started by looking at the basics of video formats, places to find free video online, followed by ways of downloading videos from YouTube and TeacherTube. We then looked at ways of extracting DVD selections for later editing, and how to create photo stories, screencasts, an online TV station, and a stop motion video. Exploring Mogulus Studio was a good introduction to online based software (sometimes called webware), and in the next chapter, on Web 2.0 tools and other multimedia forms, we will focus on the kind of tools that are very common these days. This concept, of the Web as an Operating System and Web 2.0 tools as social applications, can be a nice metaphor for learning, and can extend Moodle's possibilities by giving students more tools for creating content, and a space to reflect, discuss, and assess these creations.

5
Web 2.0 and Other Multimedia Forms

In this chapter, we will focus essentially on Web 2.0 tools for creating multimedia. Web 2.0 is a new way of working on the Web, where most of the users don't just access information but also create it—a usual metaphor is a change from a "read", more common during the early days of the Web, to a "read-write" Web. However, we will not look at blogs, wikis, or social networking sites that are usually referred to as Web 2.0 reference tools. Moodle already has these, so instead we will take a look at Web applications that allow the easy creation, collaboration, and sharing of multimedia elements, such as interactive floor planners, online maps, timelines, and many others applications that are very easy to use and that support different learning styles. Usually, I use the idea of Moodle as a schools operating system and Web 2.0 as its social applications to illustrate what I believe can be a very powerful way of using Moodle and the Web for learning. Designing meaningful activities in Moodle gives students the opportunity to express their creativity by using these tools and reflecting on the produced multimedia artifacts with both peers and teacher.

However, we have to keep in mind some issues of e-safety, backups, and licensing, when using these online tools, which are usually associated with communities. After all, we will have our students using them, and they will therefore be exposed to some risks. The last chapter of this book will deal with these issues.

By the end of this chapter you will be able to:

- Use a set of free online software tools for common procedures in multimedia creation and sharing
- Create interactive multimedia artifacts for use in course delivery
- Integrate these multimedia artifacts in Moodle

Creating gadgets to represent data by using Google Docs (Spreadsheets)

Gadgets are visual representations of data, a concept used by Google Docs, especially in the Spreadsheets tool. If you don't know Google Docs, this is a good time to learn something about it and the possibilities that it offers for education. Assigning students in our Moodle course tasks such as preparing a studio budget in *Module 6 – Spaces for Music*—will require them to use a tool like this to present their plans to their colleagues in a visual way.

Google Docs (`http://docs.google.com`) provides a set of online Office tools that work on Web standards and recreate the typical Office suite of software applications—we can make documents, spreadsheets, presentations, or more recently, forms, meaning feedback/quiz modules.

To use Google Docs, we will need a Google account. If you don't already have one, you might consider creating one by navigating to `https://www.google.com/accounts` and then clicking on the option **Create an account now**, as shown in the screenshot below:

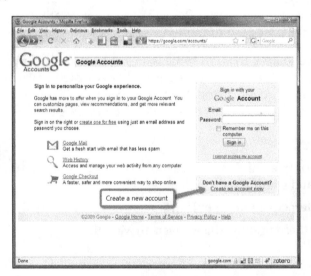

In addition to being easy and free, a Google account gives you access to a pack of online software applications, including YouTube, Google Maps, Feedburner, Blogger, Analytics, Custom search, and so on—and of course, Google Mail, which is a good way to give our students an email account (and they can use it when registering for all of the Web 2.0 tools' web sites that we will be using in this chapter). In this book, some of these tools are explored, including YouTube and Google Docs.

After creating our new account and logging in to Google Docs, we can organize these files in folders, tag them, search (of course, it's Google!), collaborate (imagine a wiki spreadsheet), export to several formats (including the usual formats for Office documents from Microsoft, Open Office, or Adobe PDF) and publish these documents online.

We will start by creating a new Spreadsheet to make a budget for a music studio which will be built during the music course by going to **New | Spreadsheet**.

Insert a Gadget

As in any spreadsheet application, we can add some equipment and costs to the cells:

After populating our table with values, instead of adding a simple **Chart**, we have a new option called **Gadget:**

If we click on this, we have several options, as shown in the screenshot below:

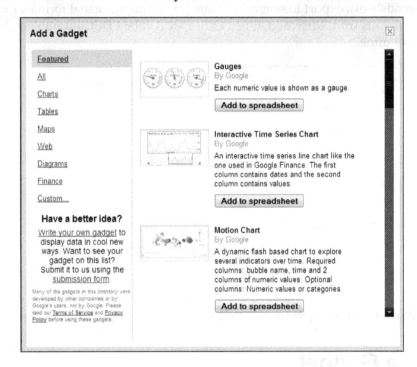

One of these is the **Pile Chart**, that shows piles of **$100 bills** according to the values in the spreadsheet.

We need to add titles to the **Gadget** and **Chart**, and then click on the **Apply and close** button.

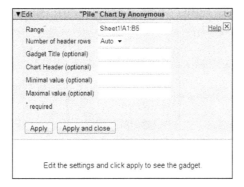

The final result will look like the following:

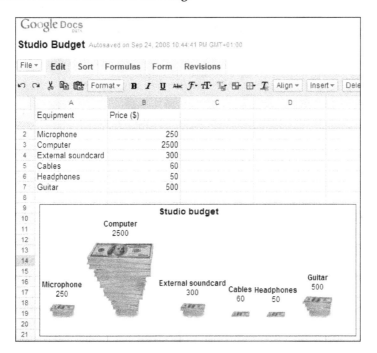

Publish

If we click on the Gadget, a grey bar will be displayed on top of it, and if we click on the drop-down arrow in the right corner, there is a **Publish Gadget...** option, which can be used to publish the gadget:

When we click on this option, embed code will be displayed; we can use this to put the gadget on a Moodle forum, as we have seen in previous chapters.

The code provided by this application (and some others that we will be using, such as Google Maps) uses the iframe or script tags. We need to make a small hack to the code, as it does not work inside forum posts in Moodle, resources and activities, summaries, and quizzes, as-is. The way to counter this is to add the <html> and </html> tags to the beginning and end of the embed code respectively, and we would have something similar to <html><iframe src="..."></html>.
Refer to the following screenshot:

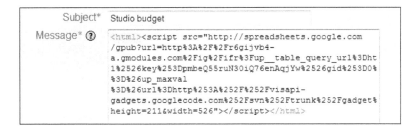

Discuss, Share, Collaborate

Google Docs offers some new possibilities, with options for discussing, sharing, and publishing available from the upper-right corner of each opened document.

The **Discuss** option allows us to chat about a document with others, as we write it. The **Share** option allows us to invite collaborators to edit our document either at the same time as we are editing it, or asynchronously. Remember that this can be quite useful in distance courses that have collaborative tasks assigned to groups.

Creating floor plans using a floor planner

Designing spaces can be an interesting activity in several subjects, starting at the conceptual stage with digital prototyping, and including trial of solutions, without a great deal of effort. We could use a floor planner to design:

- A new school laboratory
- A photography studio
- "The school we want"
- A yard
- An eco-friendly house
- An activity for language teaching, where students would have to name objects in different places
- A set for a drama performance
- A setting in which characters of a book move around in, for creative writing

In the "good old days", when computers were rare, I built a music studio with an old friend of mine. At that time we had neither the money nor the fancy digital floor planners, so we just used the usual techniques of buying cheap stuff, and trial and error, moving instruments and equipments repeatedly until we found the perfect configuration. We got egg boxes from a friend who had a cakes factory, some old carpets from a neighbor, cork and styrofoam for the doors, walls and ceiling, and an old hatch to make a window in a previously-scary, dark, and humid basement. We were thrilled with the result—a decent studio for little money. I remember we called it "Studio 2" as at that time I had a 1990 Mini with that model. That's where I got the idea for the following course activity.

In *Module 6 – Spaces for music*—following the budgeting of the studio that we saw previously with Gadgets, students are asked to create a 3D representation of the studio of their dreams, by using an online floor planner tool.

Floor Planner (`http://www.floorplanner.com`) is an online planning tool that allows us to create one floor plan for free, which can be seen in 3D and embedded anywhere, including in our Moodle courses.

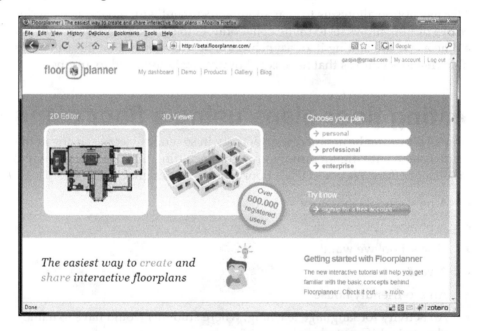

After logging in with our details, we are taken to **My dashboard**, where we can manage our account and create our first project by clicking on the **start a new project** button:

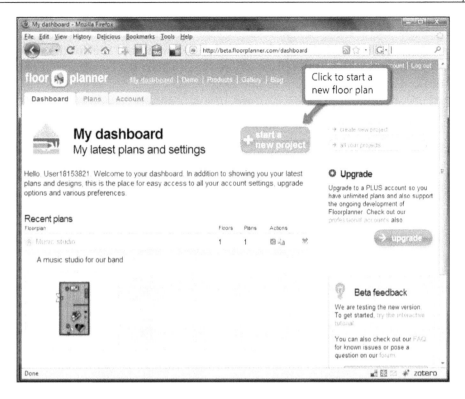

We can then start entering the details for the floor plan:

Create a room

After we are done, we need to click on the **Create plan** button. We are then presented with the workspace, which is the place where we can start the construction of our music studio. The first steps are:

1. Click on the **draw room** icon in the **Construction** menu on the right. The mouse pointer changes to a black cross..

2. Left-click in the squared area, and drag the mouse to make a rectangle of the size that you want for your studio.

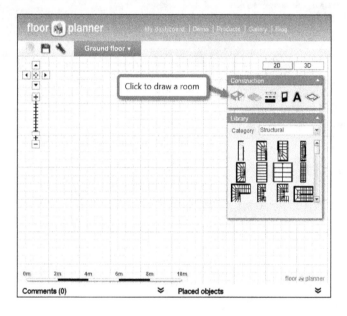

Add a floor

Now, let's add a floor to our room. We need to double-click on the surface inside the room that we've just created, and then select one of the patterns for the floor of our room from the pop-up window:

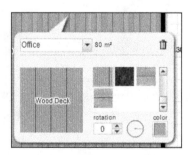

Add elements

We can now add doors, windows, and furniture to the plan. If we click on the door icon in the **Construction** toolbar, we will get a library of elements that we can drag onto the plan.

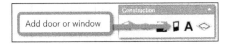

In the **Miscellaneous** category we can find some instruments for our course activity.

Save and publish

We have to make sure that we save our design before leaving the floor planner, by using the typical **Save** button located in the upper-left corner of the screen:

If we click on the **3D** button above the **Construction** toolbar, we can see the plan in a 3D view, as seen in the following screenshot:

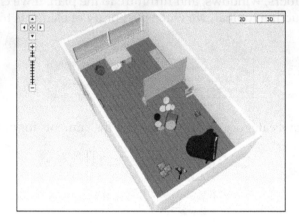

When we're done, we have at least two options in the publish menu in the upper right corner that can be useful for us to use the floor plan in Moodle:

- If we want to export the plan as an image, we need to click on the image icon (second from the left) and save the file to our computer. Because we have a free account, the maximum image size is 640x480. We can later upload this file to Moodle, as we saw in Chapter 2.

- If we want to embed or link to it from within Moodle, we can use the hyperlink icon on the rightmost side of the toolbar above and use the embed code or the given URL:

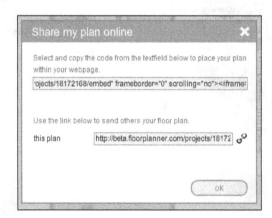

Creating mind maps using Mindomo

Mind maps are an excellent technique for students to perform connections among concepts and to help them think about subjects. They can be used as a nice revision tool as well. In our course, one of the activities in *Module 4 - Music is a language* — deals with creating a mind map about some of the music theory concepts. We will use a tool called Mindomo to create this mind map.

Mindomo (`http://www.mindomo.com/`) is an online mind map software that we can use to create multimedia mind maps, with text, videos, images, and hyperlinks.

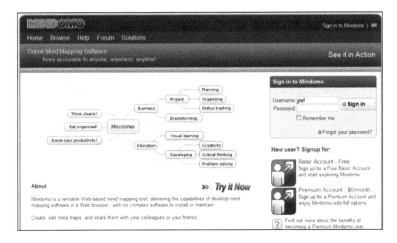

With a basic, free account we can create up to seven mind maps.

After signing up, we can create a new mind map (or even open a shared one by using the folders at the bottom) and start editing it by clicking on **Private** (to make our Mindomo just editable by us) and then on **New**, as shown in the following screenshot.

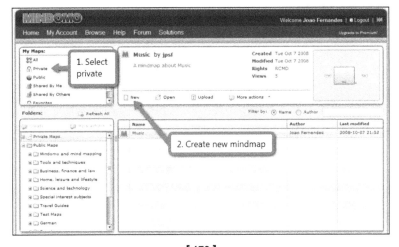

Add topics

The interface of Mindomo is very similar to Office 2007 applications, with a Ribbon menu that has several categories of functions. The most important functions for us are in the **Home** tab—the **Insert** area with the **Topic** and **Subtopic** options and the **Insert** tab, marked in the following screenshot. For now, let's start by giving the main topic a name—**Music**—and add some more topics by clicking on the **Topic** option.

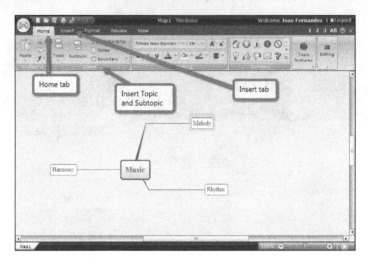

Add multimedia elements

To add videos, images, or hyperlinks, follow these steps:

1. Click on one of the **Topics** or **Subtopics** in the workspace.
2. Click on the **Insert** tab.
3. Click on the **Multimedia** option in the **Topic** features sub-tab.
4. Select the type of multimedia object that you want to add.

A sidebar is displayed on the leftmost side of the workspace, which allows us to add, for example, a video from YouTube, to illustrate some of the concepts in our mind map.

After clicking on the **Add YouTube Video** button at the bottom, we can paste the URL of the video:

We will get something similar to the following screenshot, with videos showing up inside subtopics:

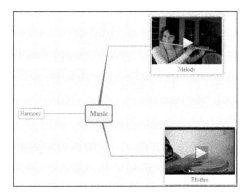

Save and publish

Finally, we can save the mind map by using the **File** menu found in the upper-left corner, which is typical of software applications.

To get the URL or embed code for Moodle integration so that we can share the mind map, there is a dedicated button (**Share**) in the same area, just to the right of the printer icon. If we click on this button, and go to the **Publishing** tab we can get both the URL and the embed code. If we click on the **Generate** button, the embed code will be copied to the clipboard, and we can then paste it in Moodle.

Creating interactive timelines using Dipity

Interactive timelines can be very useful for illustrating historical events and change through time, allowing us to have a better visual perspective on the succession of events that lead to a particular moment. From major events in your life to the history of a game, a country, a theory, a person, or a sequence of news items that came out about a subject, many uses can be thought of for this kind of tool. Now imagine adding images, audio, video, and hyperlinks to it, along with some nice navigation, and you'll realize the added value of this tool.

In our course, in *Module 1 – Music evolves* — one of the activities will require students to create timelines of particular music genres selected by them, and include audio, video, and hyperlinked references related to this genre.

Dipity (http://www.dipity.com/) is an online tool that allows us to create interactive multimedia timelines. It requires registration and is free to use, so every student can create his or her own account.

Add a topic

After creating an account, the first step is to create a new topic. To do this, carry out the following steps:

1. Click on the **My topics** tab.

2. Click on the **Add a Topic** button.

A window is displayed, and we will need to click on the **Blank** button at the top of the window, and then start completing the form with information about our timeline:

Finally, when we click on the **Create Topic** button, we will get an empty timeline, as shown in the following screenshot:

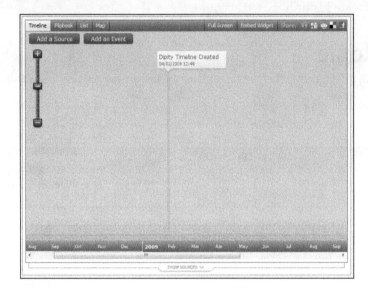

Note that we will have a default event in our new timeline, representing the moment at which the timeline was created. We can delete this later.

Add an event

We can now add new events to the timeline by clicking on the **Add an Event** button in the upper-left corner, and then completing one form, for each event:

In this form, we can insert pictures (either uploaded or from an online service), add links, a location (which will show in an online map), and also videos from online services such as YouTube. The timeline will show a new event with the picture that we have selected, as shown in the following screenshot:

If we click on the event, we will see the multimedia elements that we have added, one per tab:

Share

After adding all of the events to the timeline, we can click on the **Embed Widget** option in the upper-right corner of our timeline:

We can customize several aspects of the widget, such as its size or zoom factor, and then copy and paste the embed code into Moodle (don't forget the <html> and </html> tags around the iframe type of embed code).

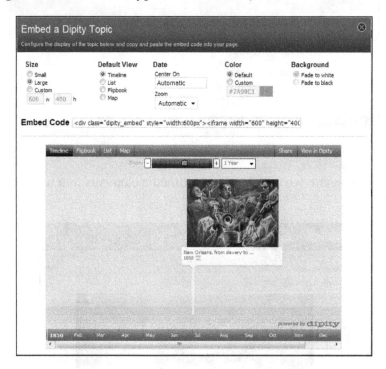

Creating custom maps using Google Maps

Accessing images from all around the world was impossible some years ago. We are talking about huge amounts of information in terms of photos taken by satellites or produced by geographers and earth scientists. Such information wasn't available to everyone in a practical way.

We will require students to create an online map in *Module 2 – A world of music*, to illustrate the geographical history of some instruments from around the world. Some of these instruments, such as the ukulele, travelled thousands of kilometers — was taken by the Portuguese sailors to Hawaii!

Google Maps (`http://maps.google.com`) is one of several online map services available that does not just allow us to search and navigate in this sea of geographical information, but also makes available various tools that make these maps more interesting for teaching and learning. These tools are placemarks, lines and areas; these are the digital equivalents of the elements we would use in real, paper-based maps to represent information about them. The advantage here again is the possibilities that multimedia brings. We can use this in activities to, for example:

- Display places of interest with multimedia placemarks (earthquakes, volcanoes, schools, animals from several biomes, historical buildings, events such as battles, and so on)

- Draw lines and areas on the maps (illustrating routes or regions, for example the trip of a Portuguese navigator such as Vasco da Gama from Portugal to India, administrative regions, or even a plan of a study visit to a nature reserve)

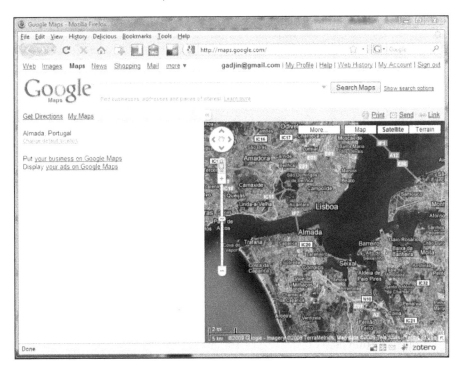

Create a new map

After we log in to our Google account, we just need to go back to Google Maps and create a new map by clicking on the **Create new map** option under the **My Maps** tab (below the Google logo):

We will now need to complete a form, giving the **Title** of the map, a **Description**, and the **Privacy and sharing settings** (**Public** in our case).

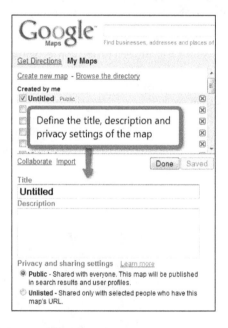

Add a placemark

Adding a placemark is very simple. The first thing to do is to find the place where we want to put it. For this we have two options:

- Drag the map in any direction with the mouse (while keeping the left mouse button pressed) and use the scroll wheel to zoom in or out, or just use the navigation interface on the left of the map.

- Perform a search by using the search form. This will automatically add a pink placemark to the location that we are searching for. This is not the placemark we want in our map, just the location, so we should click again on the **My Maps** link below the Google logo, and then add our own placemark by using the provided toolbar.

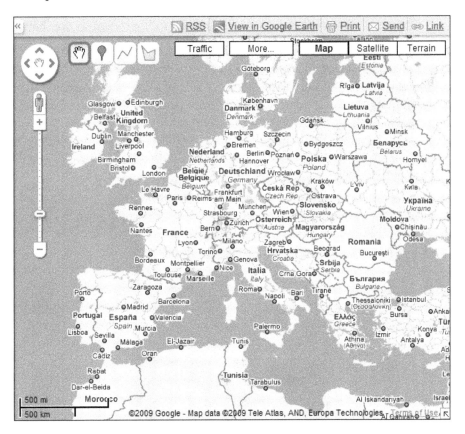

But before we add the placemark, we should be aware that we have several types of maps that we can display—either road maps, satellite imagery, terrain information, and in some cases, where available, street views and traffic information as well. To select the appropriate one, we should use the upper-right corner buttons, as shown in the following image:

And now let's take a look at the placemark. There's a toolbar for adding elements to the map on the upper-left corner of the map region, above the navigation bar:

We should click on the blue placemark button on the toolbar, next to the "hand" tool, and position it where we want to add the placemark to the map.

Now, in the provided popup, we can insert all of the information that we want to include, in the title and description fields, for example, text with some basic formatting, an image, a link, or even a video from YouTube or TeacherTube. An easy way of doing this is by using the existing rich text editor, which is a simpler version of Moodle's HTML editor. Remember that if we want to insert a TeacherTube video to our placemark, we will have to switch to HTML mode by clicking on the **Edit HTML** link and then paste the embed code there.

If we click the **OK** button, followed by the **Save** and **Done** buttons in the leftmost sidebar, and finally in the placemark, we can see the following results:

Add a line

To suggest a connection between placemarks (for example, a route), we can add lines to our map, connecting the placemarks. After clicking on the line icon in the toolbar, we just need to set a starting point by clicking on it. Next, we can click on as many additional points as we wish. In this way, a line will be drawn between the points that we select. When we are done, we just need to double click with the left mouse button.

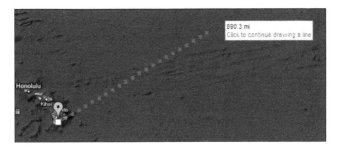

Share

In the upper-right corner of our map, we can see a **Link** option:

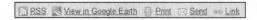

If we click on this, we get a direct link to the map (with its placemarks, lines, and regions) or the embed code. We can also customize and preview the embedded map (by clicking on the **Customize and preview embedded map** option) where we have the option of changing the size of the map, and can copy the embed code from there. I would recommend that you use this customization, get the resulting code, and then paste it into Moodle.

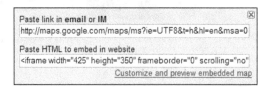

Don't forget—we are dealing with the iframe tag, and so we need to add the `<html>` and `</html>` tags around the embed code to integrate it into Moodle. All of this will result in the following:

Just a quick reference to finish this section on online maps, to Google Earth (`http://earth.google.com`). This is a computer software application that uses the same map data as Google Maps. It has more functionality than the latter (you can work in 3D, explore the Moon, Mars, and Sky maps, insert GPS data, take measurements, among others).

Creating an online presentation using Voicethread

Online presentations are a great way of providing students with the opportunity to develop their presentation skills. And I'm not just talking about creating Powerpoint-like presentations, but of presenting and discussing by using audio and video. Some uses for this can be:

- Create online presentations or discussions around slideshows, screenshots, pictures, music, or video (of a study trip, works of art, an idea, a political cartoon, an experiment, football game tactics, a trainee teacher's class, and so on)
- Create book or CD reviews
- Introduce students to each other by showing some of their photos, work, and/or videos (or to critique their own work)

The advantage of this kind of presentation is that we don't need to be at the same place at the same time to make this happen. Another advantage is that using Moodle alone for this doesn't provide the same kind of flexibility and speed of use (we would have to use a forum, do a lot of uploads of multimedia elements, and all of this multiplied by the number of students).

In our course, the context for using this tool will be a final course event, where every student will have to present his or her best works in 20 slides, with only 20 seconds to spend talking about each (their colleagues will have to comment on them, too). This presentation format is called Pecha Kucha and started in the young designers' world as a way of showing their works in an efficient way. The 20x20 format allows a total presentation time of 6:40 per person, which is enough time to show the important stuff.

Voicethread (http://voicethread.com) is a web tool that, in its own words, enables "group conversations around images, docs, and videos".

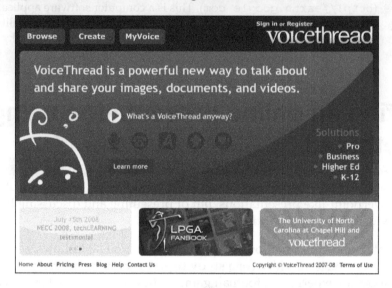

With this tool we can create online collaborative multimedia presentations that integrate images (including Flickr images), documents (PDF, Microsoft Office) and videos, allowing peers to leave comments using voice (with a microphone or telephone), text, audio (a file), or video (with a webcam). These presentations can be embedded into Moodle, or any web page.

After creating a new account in Voicethread, we can start by adding a picture to our profile. In the **My Voice** tab, in the upper-right corner, we should click on the drop-down arrow and then on **My account**, to add an image to our identity:

Upload media

Now let's start by uploading media to a new Voicethread thread, by clicking on the **Create** tab and then on one of the **Upload** options:

We can upload files from our computer (PDF, Microsoft Office, including 2007 formats), images from our Flickr or Facebook accounts, or add URLs of documents or images on the Web.

As an example, I have added a URL to a photo of Miles Davis, from Flickr:

After we click on the **(add a title and link)** link, we get the following screenshot, where I have added the title and link to the source:

We can do this as many times as required, until we have all of the material for the presentation available online.

Comment

Next, let's learn to comment on the material that we have uploaded. If we click on **Comment** in the left-hand menu, a preview of the voicethread is displayed. Here, we need to click on the **comment** button below the image:

We will be offered several options to add comments. From left to right, these are (refer to the following screenshot as well):

- Phone
- Video (webcam)
- Audio (voice from microphone)
- Text and draw (we can actually draw over pictures, slides, or even videos! This is called Doodling)
- Upload an audio file (for example, combined voice and music created in Audacity)

After we add a comment to the first slide, we can click on the 'next' arrow on the bottom right and add another comment to the next slide, and so on. A comment will be added with a thumbnail of our picture next to the slideshow, as shown in the following screenshot:

Share

Finally, it's time to add the slideshow to Moodle by getting the embed code. But before we do this, let's set some publishing options so that others can listen to our comments and join in the discussion, adding their own views. For this, click on the **Publishing Options** button at the bottom of the page:

We can allow anyone to view or comment, and set the moderation to **On** if we want to have more control over the comments (meaning that any comment for our voicethread from other users will have to be approved by us before it is published).

Finally, click on the **Save** button and then on the **Embed** button on the left, and copy-and-paste the code into Moodle!

Summary

In this chapter, we focused on activities that we can perform by using Moodle and some Web 2.0 tools. The objective was to show how this integration can open several possibilities for teaching and learning, providing free applications where teachers and students can create their own multimedia works, and then embed them in Moodle for instruction, discussion, or assessment. We created interactive floor plans, timelines, maps, online presentations, and gadgets, to represent data and mind maps. We also saw the possibilities of having collaboration in the construction of these multimedia works, as most Web 2.0 tools have a standard option to create a collective work with others. But to achieve this, we need better communication and assessment tools to complement the ones provided by Moodle, something we will see in the following chapters.

6

Multimedia and Assessments

In this chapter, we will create assessment activities using multimedia. We will use images, audio, and video to create interactive exercises, either by using Moodle's quizzes, lessons, or assignments, or by using external tools such as Hot Potatoes and JClic, which can later be integrated into our course.

By the end of this chapter you will be able to:

- Add multimedia to multiple choice answers in Moodle quizzes and lessons
- Create crosswords and jumble exercises in HotPotatoes
- Create puzzles and "find-the-pair" activities using JClic
- Integrate all of these activities into Moodle

Adding multimedia to multiple choice answers in Moodle quizzes and lessons

Sometimes it can be useful to insert multimedia elements into the answers of a multiple choice question in a Moodle lesson or quiz. This can apply to situations where students are required to:

- Recognize audio excerpts corresponding to text, images, or videos (for example, in music or language courses students have to identify a melody from a music sheet excerpt, or the correct pronunciation of a given text)
- Recognize video scenes (for example, corresponding to a certain dialogue, gestural conversation, and so on)

Adding multimedia to the question body is fairly easy because we can use the HTML editor and just link to a multimedia file, and the Moodle filter will do the rest. But adding questions for which the answer choices are multimedia files is a different story, as there is no HTML editor, just a simple text form. However, this is not complicated with the help of the correct HTML code.

For example, in the course, *Module 1 - Music Evolves*—students have to post excerpts of songs from different moments of a musical genre to a forum topic as attachments (see Chapter 3 for details on slicing audio). In the same module, we will create a quiz (**Mini-quiz – history of music**) that will use the excerpts posted by our students in its questions, as an incentive for other students to have a look at their colleagues' work.

So, after creating a new quiz and adding a new multiple choice question to it (for example, "Which of the following excerpts refers to medieval music?") we can add links to the MP3 files submitted by students as choices. We can get these links as we saw previously, by right-clicking (*CTRL+click* for Mac users) on the linked MP3 file in the forum post and then clicking on the **Copy Link Location** option, as shown in the following screenshot:

Next, while editing the multiple choice question, we can paste the link location in the answer form, for example, for **Choice 1**. This is the easy way, as Moodle, with its multimedia filter, will do the rest:

As a result, we'll get something like this:

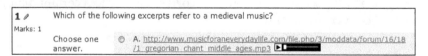

However, note that the entire link to the file shows up, which is not very aesthetically-pleasing (and can give clues to the correct answer to students in the filename). We can solve this by using a simple HREF HTML tag in the answer forms, so that we obtain something cleaner, such as this:

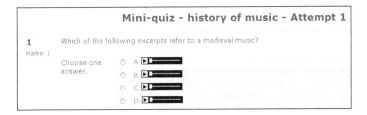

In this case, we can use the following code: `<a href="pasted link location"> link text </a>` with a SPACE in the link text:

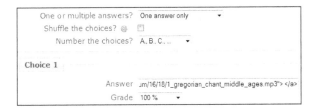

The same concept applies for videos and music from online services (TeacherTube, YouTube, Imeem, and so on) as we can paste the embed code in the answer form. In this case, there is no need to use any extra HTML code. So adding the embed code in the following manner:

will result in the following screenshot:

When using this process, we should keep in mind a couple of things:

- The multimedia files that are linked in the choice options MUST be available to the students in the course. If we copy the link location from the files area but the file is not available to the students, we'll have problems. The same applies to attachments in forum posts, with separate groups.

- Consider the situation where the files linked to in the answer options are those of an attachment in a forum post on the course. Suppose the question is shared and the quiz is restored in another course or exported to another Moodle installation. In this case, there will be problems with the file access as the hyperlink will point to the original source in a particular course, which is not currently available.

- In the case of videos or audio from online services, embedding may be disabled by request, so these can later become unavailable in the course.

- Too many links to MP3 files on the same quiz page, and/or MP3 files of considerable size can slow down the page loading.

As a possible solution to the first three issues, we can have the multimedia files in a public folder on our server. In this way, files can be accessed from different courses and domains. We could, for example, download a YouTube video and make it available on our server, if this service is blocked in our school or institution (see Chapter 4 for information on this). Another option is to upload these files to the course files area (but in this case, the files must be made available to students in the course, by using the **Display a directory** resource, or they will not have permissions to listen to or see them).

There is a trick that can be used to make content available in a course without showing it in the course topics. To do this, we can go to the course settings and add an extra topic, creating the resources and activities that we don't want to show to our students (however, everything for now should be visible, so no "eyes closed" icons!). After we're done, we should go again to the course settings and remove the extra topic. In this way, the content is there, is "visible" from a permissions point of view, but at the same doesn't show in the course. This can be a way of having the files available for quizzes and other activities.

As a possible solution to the last problem, we can use page breaks, or have one question per page in the quiz, so that students can only load one question at a time. Another solution is to reduce the file sizes, either by slicing or encoding the files in other formats. In the case of a MP3, reducing the bitrate could be an option—see Chapter 3 for information on this.

Adding multimedia to quizzes, lessons, and assignments

Remember that multimedia can be used in interesting ways in not only multiple choice answers but also in question bodies and lesson content and assignments. We can create lessons in a tutorial style, with videos followed by some questions on the video's content, leading to different lesson branches according to the answers, or assignments can be presented as quick briefing videos. And don't forget that if we want to receive multimedia assignments, we should set this activity to allow students' file uploads.

Creating exercises with Hot Potatoes

Hot Potatoes (`http://hotpot.uvic.ca`) from Half Baked Software allows us to create interactive web games and puzzles in a simple way. One of the advantages of Hot Potatoes over Moodle's quiz engine is that Hot Potatoes makes it easier to create exercises, and some of these are very different from the ones available in Moodle, for example crosswords, and finding pairs via drag and drop. The license for this software is a peculiar one, as it allows free use by individuals working for state-funded educational institutions that are non-profit making, on the condition that the material produced using the application is freely available to anyone via the Web (this means that a Moodle course without access to guests, without a key wouldn't probably qualify). Other uses require a license, so we should keep this in mind.

We need to register the software at `http://hotpot.uvic.ca/reg/register.htm`. A key will be sent to our email inbox and we can then register it going to **Help | Register** and filling in the details.

There are six different types of exercises that we can create with this software:

- JQuiz - question-based exercises
- JCloze - fill in the gaps exercises
- JMatch - matching exercises
- JMix - jumble exercises
- JCross - crosswords
- The Masher - linked exercises of the different types mentioned above

We will only take a look at the JCross and JMix exercises, as the other formats can be achieved with the question types that Moodle provides in quizzes and lessons. However, you should try them and see for yourself how easy it can be!

JCross - Crosswords

In our course, *Module 4 - Music is a language*—students have to deal with a lot of new concepts on basic music theory. A crosswords exercise can be a good way to recall some of these.

After opening Hot Potatoes and clicking on the **JCross** potato, we see the standard interface—a grid, in which we can start creating a crossword exercise. We can start by adding a title to the exercise on the leftmost pane, labeled **Title**.

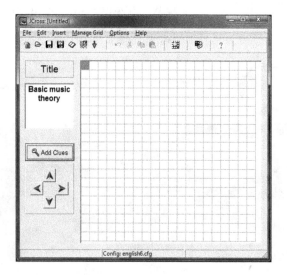

Then, we can click on the button shown in the following screenshot to **Create a grid layout automatically from a list of words**; this is the third button from the right on the toolbar:

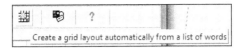

We can then **Enter each word or phrase on a separate line**, similar to the following example, and then click on the **Make the grid** button. We can also define the maximum grid size, in this case the default of 20x20 letters. When we export the exercise as HTML to include it in Moodle, this will automatically be adjusted to the size of the words in the exercise.

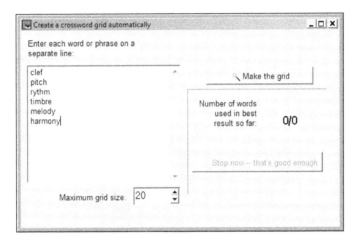

When the grid is ready, we would get something like this:

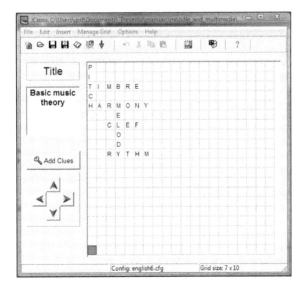

Next, we need to define the clues, just like in any crossword exercise, by clicking
on the button **Add Clues**, below the title. We will then get a list of the words in our
crosswords exercise:

Here, we just need to click on each word and add the clue in the field provided,
clicking on **OK** after specifying each clue. We can also add pictures, URLs, or other
media (videos and Flash) to the clues by using the **Insert** menu. Let's look at how to
add an image.

For the word CLEF, we could insert a picture of a bass clef so that students can see
a clue for the word. To do this, we need to select menu option **Insert | Picture |
Picture from Local File** and then select an image of a clef from our computer. Again,
remember that we need to always keep files for a single project in one folder to avoid
images disappearing when the exercise is used on different computers or on the
Web. We should first save the Hot Potatoes project in a folder, and then create an
images folder where we can put all of the images for this exercise.

So, after selecting a picture of a bass clef from our images folder, we would get the
following configuration window:

After we click on the **OK** button, our crossword exercise is ready, with the HTML code for the image already inserted:

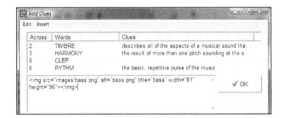

We just need to export it by pressing the *F6* key or by clicking on the button to the left of the downwards red arrow on the toolbar. We can then save it in our project folder, and preview it in the browser:

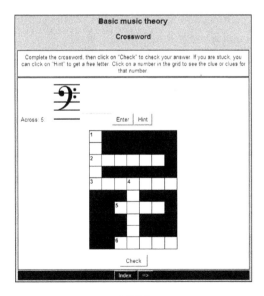

JMix - Jumble exercises

With JMix, we can create jumbled phrases or words, and students will have to put the jumbled parts into the correct order. In our course, *Module 5 - Being a musician* — students have to write about their favorite artists. We can build on this by creating a JMix exercise (or by letting students create one) that works as a review for some of the facts that they identified about these artists (again, this is an incentive for the colleagues to read what others have done).

After clicking on the JMix potato, we can start by adding a **Title** and saving our JMix file.

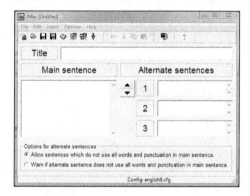

Then, in the **Main sentence** form, we can insert a sentence separated by breaks. For example, to break up the sentence "Richard Bona was born in the Cameroon in 1967" into word segments, you would type this into the main sentence box:

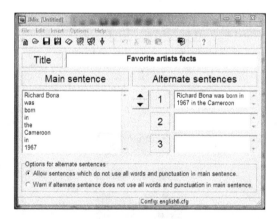

Note that in this case the phrase could be written in two ways, so there was the need to add an alternative sentence so that students can provide either answer and still be marked correct.

We can also add pictures and other multimedia elements to the title. For example, in this case we can add a photo of Richard Bona, again stored in a folder called **images**. Next, click at the end of the title that we added in the **Title** window and then go to **Insert | Picture | Picture from Local File** and select the photo from the **images** folder on our computer. To add the photo below the title, we can add a break tag , as shown below:

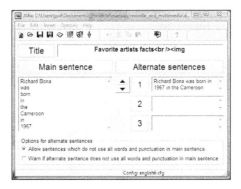

Publish

Finally, we need to export the exercise as HTML. For this type of exercise, we can export in two formats—with (*CTRL+F6* key) or without (*F6* key) the drag and drop functionality (we can also use the export buttons on the toolbar). As an example, here's the exercise with drag and drop:

Richard Bona's picture source: RV's agen (2006). Richard Bona 1.jpg. Retrieved October 10, 2008, from http://en.wikipedia.org/wiki/File:Richard_Bona-1.jpg

Moodle it!

Hot Potatoes produces an HTML file that we can add as an activity in Moodle with the same name (this activity module comes with Moodle by default but must be activated by the administrator). We just need to upload the HTML file, together with the images and other elements that we used in the exercise (for example, Richard Bona's picture), to our course files area, and then point to the HTML file from the Hot Potatoes activity settings. Let's try it with the JCross exercise that we just created. After clicking on the **Choose or upload a file...** button, we should upload the HTML file generated by the Hot Potatoes software, along with all of the multimedia files that we attached (in this case, an **images** folder and its contents) we can for example send a zip of the HTML and the folder and later unzip it in Moodle:

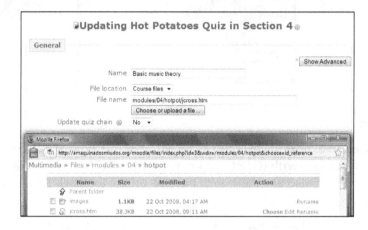

We will get a result similar to the following screenshot:

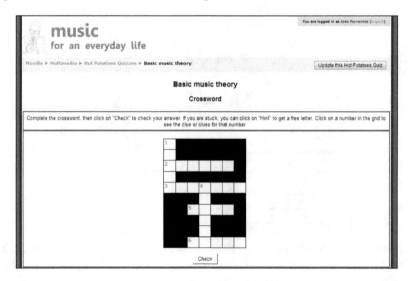

One of the advantages of integrating Hot Potatoes in this way rather than just as a resource has to do with Moodle keeping logs of students activity in the exercise, which can be of help if we want to see what they've been doing. Another advantage is the easy way of creating quizzes, when compared to Moodle's quiz engine.

Creating interactive exercises with JClic

JClic (`http://clic.xtec.net/en`) is a free (under a GPL license, more about this in Chapter 8) software application released by the Ministry of Education of the Government of Catalunya. It is written in Java, and allows us to create the following seven types of interactive activities:

- Association games - to identify the relationship between two groups of data
- Memory games - to discover hidden pairs of elements
- Exploring, Identifying, and Information games - to start with initial information and choose paths to the answer
- Puzzles – to order graphics, text, and audio, or to combine graphics and audio
- Written answers – to write text, a word, or a sentence
- Text activities – to solve exercises based on words, sentences, letters, and paragraphs (these can be completed, corrected, or ordered)
- Wordsearches and crosswords – to find hidden words or solve crossword puzzles

JClic exercises can be more visually appealing than Hot Potatoes, as we will see, and can be particularly useful for younger students. But, as they require Java, this should be checked with the ICT coordinator as Java must be installed on the schools' PCs.

In the software download area (`http://clic.edu365.cat/en/jclic/download.htm`), we can download JClic author, the application that allows us to create these activities. The file will use WebStart, and will run from a single file, named `jclic.jnlp`. When we run it for the first time, in Microsoft Vista at least, we will need to give permission for the application to **Run** (selecting the **Always trust content from this publisher** option will avoid having to perform this step every time we start JClic):

Then JClic will start loading:

The interface of JClic author is as shown in the following screenshot:

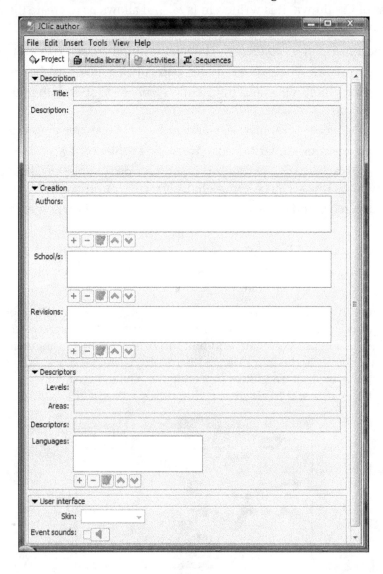

As it can be seen, there are four available tabs:

- **Project** – the default tab, which allows us to define some details of the project.
- **Media library** – where pictures and other multimedia are managed.
- **Activities** – where the project activities are created or modified. This tab further contains four tabs.
- **Sequences** – where we can sequence several activities in the same project.

The options inside these tabs will be available only after we create a new project.

Start a new project

The first step in building interactive JClic activities is to start a new project (via menu option **File | New project**):

We should then define:

- The name of the project
- The name of the file in which the project will be saved (having a double extension of `.jclic.zip`)
- The default folder for saving the files to is:

  `C:/Programme Files/JClic/projects/name of project` (in Windows)

  `$home/JClic/projects/name of project` (in other OSs)

We can change this and, if we are using multimedia files, again we should keep everything organized inside this folder.

Creating a puzzle activity

We are now ready to start creating our first activity, a puzzle. In *Module 2 - A world of music* — we can pick some of the pictures of instruments that our students gathered in the Instrument Mappers activities and create a jigsaw puzzle as part of a final game for the module. We will perform the following steps:

1. Provide details of the project in the **Project** tab.

2. Import a picture to the **Media library**.

3. Add an activity called **Exchangeable puzzle**.

4. Create a sequence.

Note that we are starting from the tab on the left and moving to the right as we configure the activity.

As an example, I created a project called **Instruments**:

Next, I added a description of the activity and specified myself as an author by clicking on the plus (+) button. We can specify in more details, but for now this much information is enough as an example.

Now, let's import a picture into our **Media library** by clicking on the icon on the far left on the toolbar:

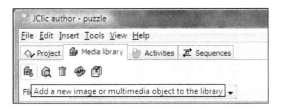

If we pick a picture from any folder on our computer, JClic will recommend that this be copied to the project folder (we should accept this recommendation, especially if we want to upload our activity to Moodle).

Note that the Media library accepts different kinds of multimedia files, from MP3 to Flash and video. This can be useful in other types of activities.

We now have a picture of a **lamelaphone** that will make a difficult jigsaw for our students.

Lamelaphone image source: Weeks, Alex (2006). Mbira dzavadzimu 1.jpg. Retrieved October 12, 2008, from `http://commons.wikimedia.org/wiki/File:Mbira_dzavadzimu_1.jpg`

The next step is to add the puzzle activity, on the **Activities** tab, by clicking on the icon on the far left of the toolbar:

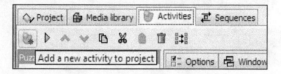

A dialog box is displayed, and in this menu we should select the **Exchange puzzle** option, entering a name for our puzzle, in the input field at the bottom of the dialog box:

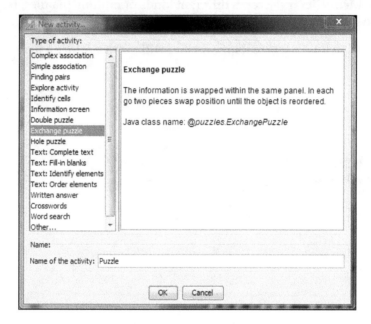

We can then add a description of the activity, and if needed, we can define a timer countdown (in the **Counters** section), among other options:

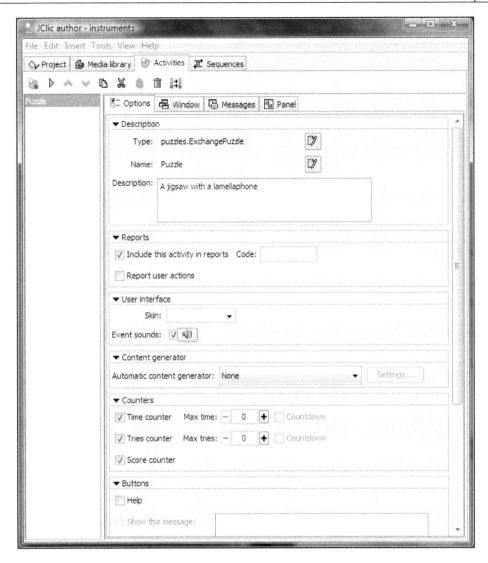

 Reports are mentioned in this dialog box. JClic provides a way to gather students' responses, but due to the complexity of this functionality, we will not deal with it in this book.

In the **Window** tab, on the the **Activities** tab, we can also define some color options, as shown in the screenshot below:

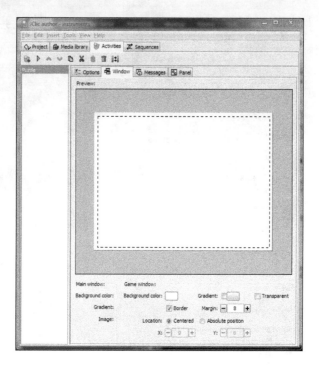

In the **Messages** tab, we can add an initial message, which for example, gives the context of the activity, and a final message, as feedback for the exercise by clicking on the dark gray areas:

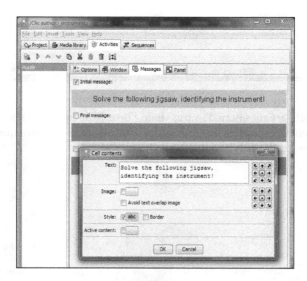

Finally, in the **Panel** tab, we should insert the lamelaphone picture from our Media library and define the kind of jigsaw that we want. In the following screenshot, I have done the following three things:

1. Selected a jigsaw with curved unions.
2. Defined 5x5 pieces.
3. Selected the image from the Media library.

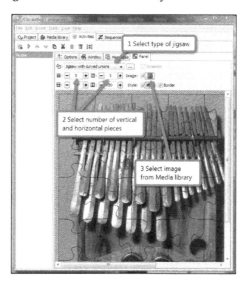

Our puzzle activity is now ready, and we can now add a finding pairs activity to the same project, in a sequence.

Creating a finding pairs activity

Finding pairs activities (where students have to locate pairs of similar pictures or in ear training exercises) can be interesting for memory exercises, and in our course in particular. In this example, students have to pick pairs of sounds with the same note from different world instruments.

After adding a new finding pairs activity (using the same process that we saw previously, for the puzzle), we should add MP3 files of the instrument sounds to our Media library. After this, in the **Panel** tab we can define the size of the grid (in this case a 3x3 grid) and then start associating the MP3 files to each cell in the grid. To do this, carry out the steps shown below:

1. Click on one of the cells in of the grid.
2. Click on the **Active content** button (similarly, if we wanted to add images, we would use the **Image** button instead).

3. In the pop-up window, click on the **Play sound button** and then select the sound file from the Media library.

4. Click on the **OK** button.

5. In the text box, add the letter of the note, just as a reference that this cell has been populated (we will delete this reference in step 7. We need to do this because we are dealing with sounds in this edit mode. With images or text it would be easier as we would have a visual reference).

6. Click on the **OK** button.

7. Remove the reference text in the text boxes from all of the rectangles.

Now, in the **Layout** tab, choose the position of the pair of this grid (the one that we edited is grid A; this can appear on the left, right, top, or bottom of the automatically created grid B). Students will have to connect an element on one grid with the similar element on the other grid.

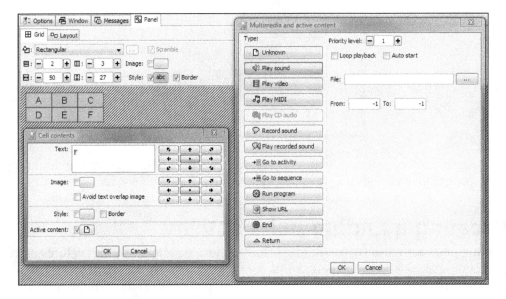

Sequencing activities

Finally, we will need to sequence the activities that we have just created. On the **Sequences** tab, if we click on the **Play** button, we will see a preview of the selected activity. This will be added automatically to the sequence list.

Note that we can either show or hide the navigation buttons in our sequence by using the options in the right-hand pane.

We can add more activities to the sequence by clicking on the button on the far left of the toolbar:

We are now ready to publish the project and add it to Moodle.

Publish

To publish the activity as a Web page, we just need to select menu option **Tools | Create web page...**. In the configuration window that is displayed, we just need to click on **OK** and then **Save**:

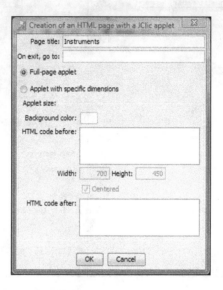

As a result, we will have an `index.htm` file and a `.jclic.zip` file, both ready to be uploaded to Moodle:

Moodle it!

In Moodle, we can now add a resource, which is a link to a file or website, and upload both files, `index.htm` and `instruments.jclic.zip` to the course files (we don't need to upload these files to the same folder).

This resource should point to the `index.htm` file, and to keep Moodle navigation visible, we should select this option in the resource settings:

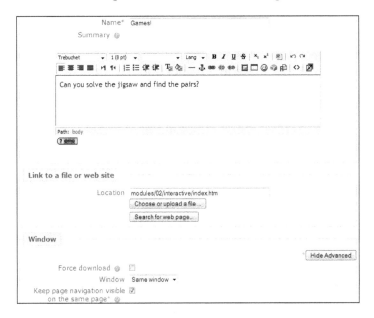

And the final result is as shown in the following screenshot:

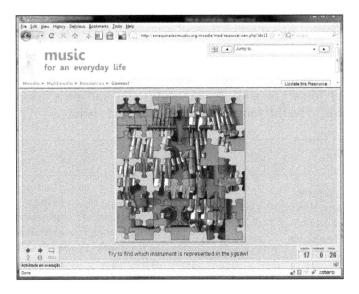

We can also design an activity where groups of students can create games like these for each other.

Assessing multimedia using rubrics

A rubric is a scoring tool that lists the criteria by which a work will be assessed, along with the several levels of achievement for these criteria. In some countries this can be defined by an exam board, while in others, it's left to the school to decide. In either case, this is a great way of providing students with the assessment criteria in which they are expected to achieve in advance and make the work of teachers easier, as the scoring is very quick. A rubric could look something like the following:

Criteria/ Level	1	2	3	4	Score
Criteria 1	Description of characteristics of the work reflecting a low level of performance in the criteria.	Description of characteristics of the work reflecting an intermediate level of performance in the criteria.	Description of characteristics of the work reflecting a high level of performance in the criteria.	Description of characteristics of the work reflecting the highest level of performance in the criteria.	
Criteria 2	...	...	...	...	

As an example of a rubric to assess the activity "My favorite artist" in *Module 5 – Being a musician*—where students have to create a photo story of their favorite artist—Level 1 in Criteria 1 (Use of images) might define the lowest level of performance as "The pictures are unrelated to the content and don't enhance understanding of the content, or are distracting and create a busy feeling" contrasting with level 4 which might be defined as"The images help in presenting an overall theme with a high impact message that appeals to the audience, demonstrating an excellent synthesis". The full range is shown in the table below.

Criteria/ Level	1	2	3	4	Score
Use of images	The pictures are unrelated to the content and don't enhance understanding of the content, or are distracting and create a busy feeling.	Description of characteristics of the work reflecting an intermediate level of performance in the criteria.	Description of characteristics of the work reflecting a high level of performance in the criteria.	The images help in presenting an overall theme with an high impact message that appeals to the audience, demonstrating an excellent synthesis.	

Now, how do we score a work from a rubric? We just need to score it according to the several criteria that we have considered, according to the levels of performance, and then apply a simple formula:

$$\text{Final classification} = \frac{\text{Total score} \times \text{the scale in which we want the final classification}}{\text{number of levels to be considered} \times \text{the number of criteria used in the rubric}}$$

Here is an example:

We want to assess a work that is being scored in five criteria, each one with four levels of possible performances, and we want the final result in a scale of 0 to 100:

Criteria	Score (1 to 4)
Criteria 1	2
Criteria 2	3
Criteria 3	3
Criteria 4	4
Criteria 5	2
Total Score	14

So the final classification will be:

$$\text{Final classification} = \frac{(14 \times 100)}{(4 \times 5)} = 70$$

Criteria

Here is a list of criteria that can be useful when assessing multimedia works:

- Design
- Content
- Organization
- Navigation
- Technical aspects (such as lighting, pace, timing, exposure, color scheme, video continuity, formats)
- Links (for example, in mind maps)
- Referencing
- Collaboration/Teamwork

Using an online spreadsheet such as Google Spreadsheets can be a good way of keeping records of our students' assessments according to these rubrics. We can obtain the final scores easily by applying formulas to cells, and can later publish them on the course page or by using Moodle's gradebook. As this tool allows collaboration, if we have students as editors, they can also perform verification work and/or peer assessments.

Summary

In this chapter we looked at integrating multimedia elements into assessment activities in Moodle, such as quizzes, lessons, and assignments and we saw the particular case of how to add multiple choice multimedia answers to quizzes and lessons. We also considered two applications, Hot Potatoes and JClic, both of which are capable of not only producing different type of exercises such as crosswords or image puzzles, but also of facilitating the construction of quizzes. The activities created with these applications were later integrated in Moodle, in the first case using a dedicated activity into Moodle, and in the second by linking to the HTML file generated by JClic. Finally, we considered rubrics as an easy way of assessing multimedia works, considering some criteria that can be used to perform this task either by teachers or students. And as the assessment is already done, we are very close to the end!

Synchronous Communication and Interaction

7

In this chapter, we will see how we can interact with our students in real time, specifically by using an online talk service and a desktop sharing application. These can be helpful for distance education, providing new ways of communicating and interacting with our students (and between them) when we are not all in the same physical space. Because Moodle does not provide effective synchronous communication tools (the chat activity could overload the server), the aforementioned tools are presented as extensions that can support our courses, giving them a new level of interaction. In distance courses with considerable duration, such communication can be a motivation and a way of providing support to students when we are online at the same time.

By the end of this chapter you will be able to:

- Use text, audio, video chat and conferencing to support communication and collaboration in Moodle courses
- Share your desktop and a collaborative whiteboard with students, supporting distance interaction in real-time in Moodle courses

Communicating in real-time using text, audio, and video

Google Chat is a service from Google that allows text, audio, and video chat amongst Google Mail users. This means that we need a Google account, something that we saw in a previous chapter.

The audio conversation is usually called **Voice over IP (VoIP)**, but as bandwidth allowances increase, the use of video is becoming common. With this tool we can:

- Meet with colleagues or students, individually or in groups
- Participate in a distant event (for example, attend a conference)
- Conduct interviews
- Teach how to play an instrument (by using the webcam)
- Teach gestural language (by using the webcam)

I find it really useful to use VoIP in distance courses, not only to give feedback to students and get to know them better, but also to create opportunities for students to interact with each other during group tasks outside of these tutor-students meeting times.

A good time to use this application is in *Module 10 – What's good music* — a theme that fits well with an online debate about how to define quality criteria for music. Students will be required to work in groups and debate on what they think is good music and how it can be assessed. This discussion will be facilitated by using this tool.

Chat and group chat

The chat option is available in Google Mail, on the sidebar on the left.
For a start, we can configure some settings, especially privacy settings, by going to **Options | Chat settings...**:

In the section **Auto-add suggested contacts**, we should select the option **Only allow people that I've explicitly approved to chat with me and see when I'm online** option, as shown in the screenshot below:

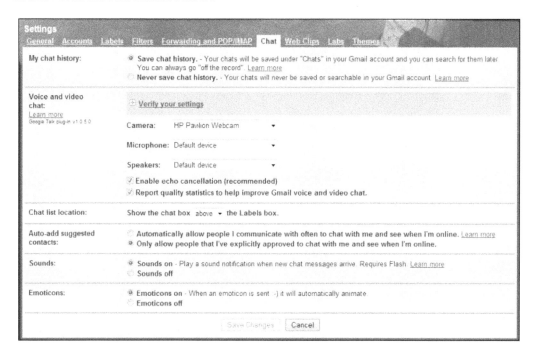

We can also disable chat history if we don't want to keep a record of our chat. There is another option during a chat to go "off record", meaning that if the chat history is on, this portion of the conversation (that takes place whilst this option is selected) will not be archived.

We are now ready to start a chat. We can search for contacts in the same Google Mail Chat sidebar, using the search form that is available (**Search, add or invite**) and double-click on the name of the contact that is displayed, or in the **Chat** link of the pop-up window that is displayed:

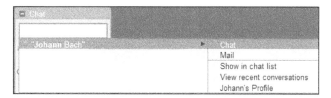

> Because the chat is synchronous, it's obvious that the (two or more) people chatting must be online. We can check if a person is online or not by looking at the small icon next to the people we've located, or in our chat list. If they have a grey, round icon on the left of their name, they are offline (or invisible and don't want to be bothered). If the color is green (available), yellow (idle), or red (busy) it's possible to chat to them.
>
> In the pop-up, we can also add the person to the chat list below the search form.

After starting the chat, a window similar to the one shown below opens in the lower-right corner of the Google Mail account, and we can start talking:

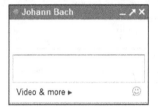

When we are chatting with someone, we can click on the **Video & More | Group Chat** option to invite one or more friends to join the conversation:

A new window will appear, in which we can chat with the participants.

Note that if we click on the arrow in the blue bar at the top of our chat window, the window will pop-up from its position in the Google Mail window and we can access it as an independent window.

If we paste a URL from a YouTube video into the chat window, a preview of the video will be integrated directly into our conversation, as shown in the screenshot below:

Transferring files

The easiest way to send files to participants for reading, or supporting discussion or commenting upon is either by using Google Mail, or by uploading them to Moodle or Google Docs and sharing these with the chat participants. This can be useful in many online discussions.

Voice and video chat

Chat, as we saw, is available by default in Google Mail, on the leftmost sidebar. To add audio and voice capabilities to this chat, we have to install a plug-in that is available at `http://mail.google.com/videochat`, for Windows and Mac users (again, sorry to Linux users).

After installing this plug-in, we can start an audio or video conversation (only one-to-one). If our contacts have a camera or microphone, we can click on the **Video & more** option again, and the following two options will be available:

In the case of voice chat, a call will be started, and we will also keep the text chat functionality:

In the case of video chat, the same applies. In the upper area, a video of the person that we are chatting with will be displayed, and in the lower corner, if we have a webcam, our video will be displayed:

Image source: Scmoewes (2005). Jimi. Retrieved March 30, 2009,
from http://www.flickr.com/photos/cmoewes/30989105/

For distance courses or even in e-learning, Google chat is an option. But if we need more complex functionality, including audio conferencing and desktop sharing, there are other tools that are available. We will now look at one in particular, called Dimdim.

Creating an online real-time classroom

A VoIP tool is great for distance education but it doesn't let you, for example, share your desktop or present a slideshow to all of the students at the same time. Dimdim (http://www.dimdim.com), an online tool for web meetings, has all of this and more, in addition to the audio and video communication possibilities, and it's free for up to 20 meeting attendants. With a tool like this we can:

- Demonstrate how to use a particular software
- Make online presentations to the entire class, with real-time annotations, using Microsoft Powerpoint, PDF files, or by sharing our entire desktop
- Draw and comment on a collaborative whiteboard

In our course, we could use this in several modules, but it would fit well in *Module 4 - Music is a language*. In this module, students have to create basic rhythms, harmonies, and melodies using free software, so that as a teacher we can discuss some of the basic music theory and use of applications to create music, sharing our desktop, in particular by using applications such as Finale Notepad or Hydrogen.

Setting up a meeting

We can sign up for free and start a meeting in Dimdim by carrying out a few simple steps. Once on the front page, we need to click on the orange button that says **Sign up Free** to create an account and, when we are ready to start our meeting, click on the green **Start Meeting** button.

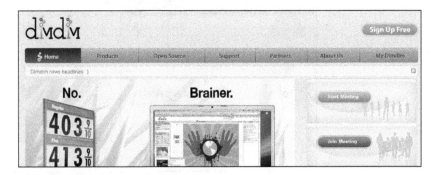

After we click on the **Start Meeting** button, a settings window is displayed:

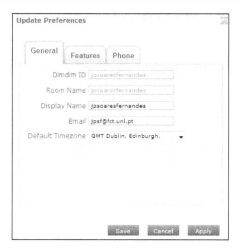

In the **General** tab, we can change our display name, email, and timezone.

In the **Features** tab, we can for example, define the length of the meeting and the return URL to which attendees should be redirected after they leave the meeting.

When we are done we just need to click the on the **Save** button, and we will be taken to **MyDimdim**:

We can now create our meeting by clicking on the **Host Meeting** button on the left. Again, we will see a settings window:

We can define the **Meeting Name** and **Agenda**, and a **Meeting Key** (which is similar to an enrolment key in Moodle). However, the best way to connect this online room to Moodle is by getting the URL to the room and adding it as a hyperlink in our course. We will see how to do this in a moment.

The **Features** tab here is similar to the one that we saw previously. In the **Phone** tab we can find a phone number and passcode that attendees can use to join the conference using a regular phone!

Finally, Dimdim will make a check of our operating system, browser, and Flash plugin, to ensure that our system is capable of hosting the meeting:

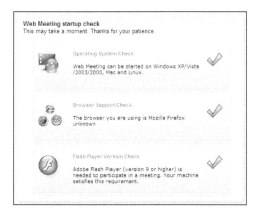

If everything's works fine, we will be taken to the main interface of the web meeting:

This interface has five main elements:

- **Items and participants** – on the left, this allows us to control what is being presented, and the participants in the meeting
- **Video Broadcaster** – this shows a video of the webcam
- **Presentation window** – in the center, this shows what is being shared with other participants
- **Public Chat** - this is a general chat area where any participant can post messages
- **Options** – in the upper right corner, this allows us to define several settings

When we connect to this online meeting space for the first time, we will need to allow Dimdim to use our webcam and microphone through the Flash Player, by clicking on the **Allow** button in the following pop-up window:

The first thing we need to do is provide the **Meeting URL** to students so that they can join the meeting. If we click on **Meeting info** in the **Options** menu, we can copy the URL and paste it into Moodle, as a resource or in a forum.

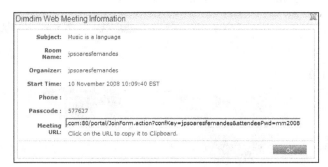

After our students start joining, we can begin the meeting.

Starting a meeting

We have three options for making presentations:

- Share our desktop
- Use a whiteboard (collaboratively or not)

- Upload a Microsof Powerpoint presentation or a PDF and use it in like a regular classroom

Sharing the desktop

To share our desktop, we will need to install the **Screencaster** plug-in. When we click on this option, we, as presenter (participants don't need to do this), will be asked to install it:

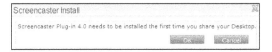

By using this plug-in, participants will see what's going on on our desktop, and we can augment this with chat (text, audio, or video), a functionality that is also included in Dimdim and we will see in a moment.

Using the whiteboard

By using the whiteboard, which is by default collaborative, we can draw with a set of tools that are available on at the right. These allow writing, drawing, stamping, and highlighting.

Uploading a Microsoft Powerpoint presentation or Adobe PDF document

In the **Share** option in the items block that we can see in the upper-left corner of the Dimdim screen, we can send a document, in Microsoft Powerpoint or Adobe PDF format, and add annotations to it while we are presenting it.

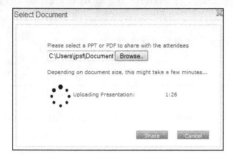

Here is an example of an uploaded PowerPoint file, with the annotations tools shown on the right:

 If we wanted, for example, to annotate a picture, the best thing to do is to insert that picture on a PowerPoint file and then share it.

Managing communication and participation

Interacting with students in Dimdim can be achieved in several ways:

- Using the public chat window on the right
- Giving audio privileges to participants
- Using the private chat to talk to individual participants
- Giving presenter privileges to participants

For this, we just need to click on the drop-down arrow next to a participant's name and select one of the options according to what we want to do. Note that simultaneous audio is only available for three users when using a free account.

We can also broadcast our webcam capture, as presenters.

Recording

Dimdim has a record functionality that keeps a copy of the meeting (except audio from students and whiteboard activity). We can use the **Record** button at the top of the presentation window for this. This can also be a way of recording performances that students might be shy to perform directly in front of their peers, or to help them in practicing for important tasks, for example, an interview.

Summary

In this chapter, we have seen two ways of adding real-time communication and interaction to our Moodle course, firstly by using VoIP, and secondly by using a web meeting tool. This interaction can be very useful, particularly for allowing students to communicate with each other and with the teacher. For distance education, synchronous tools solve several problems that come from students being in different locations, allowing us to share desktops, presentations, whiteboards, and chat.

8
Common Multimedia Issues in Moodle

In this chapter, we will discuss some common issues in using the several kinds of multimedia elements that we have discussed so far in our courses. In particular, this chapter considers copyright issues and referring to sources, Internet safety (as our students will be using Web 2.0 tools in broader communities, and this has risks), and discusses some issues with regard to Web 2.0 applications, such as backups. Finally, we will see some Moodle modules and plug-ins that can be interesting if we want to extend Moodle's multimedia capabilities.

Copyright issues

When using multimedia works that have been created by others and that are not licensed under a Creative Commons or similar license (a license in which the author grants others the right to use the work under certain conditions), we should assume that the work is an **All rights reserved** creative work. This means that almost all use of it is protected by law (for example, for the United Kingdom refer to `http://www.copyrightservice.co.uk/copyright` and for the United States of America, refer to `http://www.copyright.com/ccc/viewPage.do?pageCode=cr10-n`), and only the copyright author is allowed to make copies, distribute, translate, adapt, and perform other transformative uses for the works. However, there are some limited uses that the law allows, that fit under the "fair use" umbrella. And if we are lucky, the work is in the Public domain, which is another kind of status which means that we won't have a problem in using it! Let's see what these two concepts mean.

Fair use

"Fair use" of a copyrighted work consists of using it for a limited and "transformative" purpose. This doesn't mean that we can make copies of an entire book or code and give it to our students, because we are teaching and we have an excuse (that doesn't sound fair does it?). So, there are some aspects to keep in mind that limit this label of fair use:

- The purpose and character of our use of the work - if it is to comment, criticize, parody, news report, or teach, then we can use it
- The nature of the copyrighted work – if it is a highly-creative work or just factual, there will be more stringent limitations on the use of the work
- The amount and substantiality of the portion of the work taken by us – if we are using an acceptable sample of the work, this will not put at risk interest in the entire work (a 10% rule usually applies to fair use)
- The effect of our use of the work upon the potential market – if it loses market share due to our use of it, then it's not fair use

These guidelines give room for interpretation, but if we keep them in mind (for example, just use short clips from a video, something like 10%, and keep it private in your Moodle course, and do not publish it, for example, on TeacherTube or other Web services), it will almost certainly qualify as fair use. I can't personally guarantee this because I'm not a judge; I just know the above guidelines and follow my common sense. For example, because the course *Music for an everyday life* is freely-accessible on the Web, I avoided using copyrighted works in this way. There are copyright charts produced by several organizations with more specific guidelines, such as `http://www.halldavidson.net/copyright_chart.pdf`, that can be helpful. Check also the video A Fair(y) Use Tale at `http://www.youtube.com/watch?v=CJn_jC4FNDo` about this issue.

Bear in mind that we can always ask the copyright owner if we can use his or her work in a specific context. This can take time, but if we really want to use a substantial part of the work, this is the safest way to do it!

This is something that we can discuss with our students, as they, too, will be using other people's works to make their own. This can raise issues of social justice, the nature of creativity as an incremental process, and why some things should be free, no matter what.

Public domain

We can use any work that is in the Public domain without obtaining the permission of the original author or copyright owner. A work qualifies as being in the Public domain when:

- The copyright term has expired, or the copyright protection for that work was not maintained in a manner that was essential

- The work is an unpublished work and special rules indicate that it has fallen into the public domain

- The author or copyright owner has dedicated the work to the public domain

We can find a lot of works in the Public domain in Wikimedia Commons (`http://commons.wikimedia.org`) and the Internet Archive (`http://www.archive.org`). All of the classical music before the 19th century is in the Public domain, and all of the works published in the United States before 1923 (as of 2008) also qualify. In one of the activities in our course that we saw in Chapter 3, classical music examples that fitted this categorization were used.

There is a nice comic book about these two concepts, *Tales from the Public Domain*, that you should take a look at:

Source: Aoki, K., Boyle, J. & Jenkins, J. (2006). Bound by law?. Retrieved on February 17, 2009, from `http://www.law.duke.edu/cspd/comics`

Licensing your work under a Creative Commons license

Creative Commons (`http://creativecommons.org`) is a non-profit corporation whose mission is to make it easier for people to share and build upon the work of others. For this, it has created a set of licenses that provide authors with standardized permissions that they can attach to their digital works, informing users of the author's work on what they can and cannot do with this work.

With the possibilities of digital media, it's easier for everyone to remix and create something new from the work of others. If we depended on author permissions or fair use rules, the process would be slower (as we saw, if no license is associated to a work, we have to assume that a work is an **All rights reserved** work, with all of the restrictions inherent to this). Creative Commons is a way of accelerating the process.

Creative Commons licenses are used quite a lot on the Web today, being applied to blogs, websites, photos in Flickr, and more recently, YouTube videos, just to name a few examples.

There are four permissions that are contained in Creative Commons licenses:

- Attribution (by) - requires users to attribute a work to its original author. This covers all of the licenses

- Share-alike (sa) - a copyleft requirement that requires that any derived works be licensed under the same license

- No derivatives (nd) - where authors restrict modification

- Non-commercial (nc) - requires that the work is not used for commercial purposes

So we can license, for example, a worksheet that we created for a class, with an Attribution-Noncommercial, which would only restrict the sale of this worksheet if a profit is involved. We would, in this case, attach the logo for this particular license to the work, as shown below.

We should also add a link to the license, for example, `http://creativecommons.org/licenses/by-nc/3.0`:

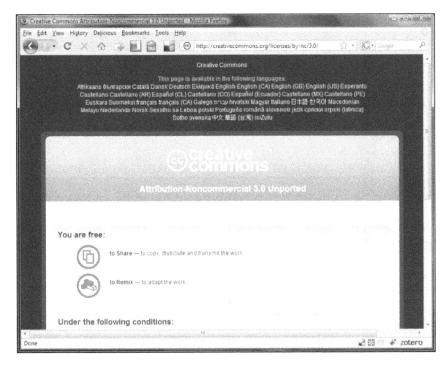

The course *Music for an everyday life* was licensed in this way, using a Creative Commons Attribution 3.0 license. You will notice the logo and the link in the footer of the course.

To select a Creative Commons license for our work (this also means our students), we can go to http://creativecommons.org/license and create the license that we want to use, and then add the license to the multimedia work (for example, either in the page where our work will be made available or at the end of a movie):

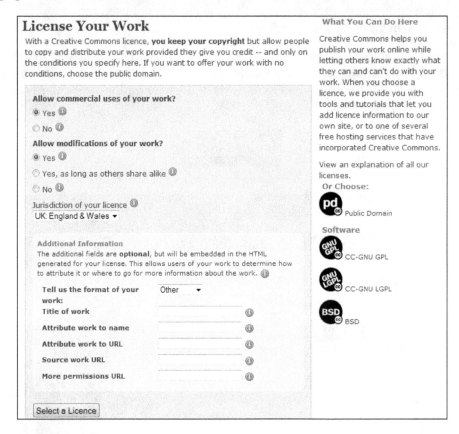

Again, bear in mind that if we don't attach any license to our works, this means it will be considered by law as an **All rights reserved** work. In this case, we might want to add our contact information to the work so that others can contact us and ask for specific permissions to reuse it.

There are other licenses that we can use when making our works available for others to build upon, such as the GNU Free Documentation License—a license by the Free Software Foundation, as used in Wikipedia. This is a "copyleft" license, meaning that derivative works should keep the same license. The **GPL** (**General Public License**) has the same concept, but specifically applies to software.

Referencing sources

In a digital world, referencing the sources that we use in our works is fundamental, not just from an ethical perspective, but also to inform others of where we found the sources, so that they can find them easily too, and use them if they wish. In a way, a reference is a link, and can be used to find something that we found interesting or inspiring.

There are several ways to reference a source, using different standards defined by institutions such as the **APA** (**American Psychological Association**). To cite a podcast for example, made by me and my editors, about writing a book without burning out, that was made available at `http://musicforaneverydaylife.com` on the 1st of February and accessed the next day on the same webpage, I would write the following reference:

Fernandes, J., Barnes, D., Mehta, N., Mangalore, S. & Shejwal, R. (2009, February 1). Writing a book without burning out – tips and techniques. Retrieved February 2, 2009, from `http://musicforaneverydaylife.com`.

Plagiarism

Plagiarism can become hard to detect in a multimedia content. Previously, in exclusively textual works, we could copy an excerpt of the work and Google it to see if there were similar texts on the Web. With music, voice, or video this can't be done so easily (tags can help, though) and as much as the activities that we design for our students are meaningful and extremely interesting, deadlines can lead to students plagiarizing other people's work. Discussing this from time to time, communicating expectations, making consequences clear, encouraging oral presentations of their work, and questioning them on how they developed their ideas, can minimize this.

Seeking further advice

There are some places to go and ask for further advice on copyright issues:

- The librarian at our school, university, or community can usually help
- The guide to copyright licensing in schools by the Schools Working Group of the Rights Industry Forum is available at `http://www.licensing-copyright.org`

- The APA Reference Style Guide by Waikato University in New Zealand is available at `http://www.waikato.ac.nz/library/learning/g_apaguide.shtml`
- The code of best practices for fair use in media literacy education is available at `http://www.centerforsocialmedia.org/resources/publications/code_for_media_literacy_education`

Safety issues

As we use the Web, especially when using online communities to post some of our multimedia works, there are some safety issues to keep in mind, and we should ALWAYS inform our students about these. This can be done during class, and reinforced by a school's policy (an acceptable usage policy, which can be connected to other policies on certain issues such as bullying or plagiarism). Some safety issues that we should be aware of are listed below.

Personal details

Personal details are sensitive information that can be used by people with bad intentions to establish contact with people, bully them, or even to steal online identities. Depending on their age, our students should keep their details to a minimum (no MSN contacts, no mobile phone, and so on) when creating accounts in online communities and should avoid publishing photos of themselves and their colleagues without their parents permission and to never arrange meetings with strangers through the Web.

Cyber-bullying

Sometimes, the Web can be used to intimidate or threaten people. It might happen that in a community, in Moodle, or through e-mail, colleagues or others bully one of our students, using threatening messages. We can only prevent this by discussing ethical issues with our students, and by being aware of changes in behavior or students' comments, working with parents to solve this. For parents, a good practice is to place the computer that is connected to the Web at home in a shared area, and to engage in conversations about their children's activities on the Web (and to participate in them!). Often, schools now create a parent's login so that they can see what their children are doing in Moodle. This is explained in detail in *Moodle Administration* by Alex Buchner, another Packt Publishing book.

Seeking further advice

There are some websites and organizations that can help us to address e-safety with our students, providing interesting resources and training such as:

- Developing an e-safety policy, by the UK's government agency BECTA (`http://schools.becta.org.uk/index.php?section=is&catcode=ss_to_es_pp_pol_03`)

- The thinkuknow website (http://www.thinkuknow.co.uk), which is published by the Child Exploitation and Online Protection Centre

- Wisekids (`http://www.wisekids.org.uk`)

- Childnet International (`http://www.childnet-int.org`)

Selecting Web 2.0 applications

When selecting Web 2.0 applications to use in our courses, there are some issues that we should be aware of. We already saw some privacy and safety aspects of this, so now let's have a look at some other aspects of it:

- Ownership and licensing – The ownership of the works that we make available online should remain ours. With regard to licensing, the company that manages the Web application has the right to distribute our work (of course, this makes sense). The license that we provide to them shouldn't be too unrestricted, though. Always check the **Terms of Service** for this. There should also be tools to enable us, as authors, to attach a license to our works (as is the case with Flickr).

- Formats – Services that use PNG, JPEG, Flash Video, MPEG-4, MP3, and all of the Web standards should be acceptable (HTML, XML, RSS).

- Backup – All of the services should have a backup facility, or facilitate this in some way, especially if editing is performed online (as is the case with online video subtitling). If it's about sending our own files, we should always keep a copy on our computer or another media.

- The level of activity of the community and development team – High levels of participation, both from the participants of the community and the development team (for example, check the company's blogs) is usually a good sign. And of course, a larger community exponentially increases the number of potential relationships.

Never forget to read the Terms of Service of a Web application or community before joining it! This is particularly true when working with students, as some applications and communities can also have age restrictions attached to them.

Moodle modules and plug-ins of interest

At `http://moodle.org/modules`, we can find many modules and plug-ins submitted by developers from around the world. Because this is a book about Moodle and multimedia, here is a short list of modules and plug-ins relating to multimedia:

- **Lightbox gallery activity module** – Allows us to create photo galleries in Moodle. Get it from `http://moodle.org/mod/data/view.php?d=13&rid=1021`

- **Stamp activity module** – Allows providing stamps to students, just like those on a paper saying "Well done!" Get it from `http://moodle.org/mod/data/view.php?d=13&rid=1338`

- **Skype activity module** – Allows us to use Skype in our course, enabling video calling, file sharing, SMS and chat with our participants. Get it from `http://moodle.org/mod/data/view.php?d=13&rid=1108`

- **Dimdim activity module** – Allows us to use Dimdim in our course, enabling web meetings with screen and whiteboard sharing with our participants. Get it from `http://moodle.org/mod/data/view.php?d=13&rid=932`

- **Application filters** – If we use the following software with our students, there are filters that automatically display the files created in these, when linked into any content in Moodle:

    ○ Geogebra – A geometry application - `http://www.geogebra.org/cms`. Get it from `http://moodle.org/mod/data/view.php?d=13&rid=585`

    ○ Netlogo – A modeling tool based on the Logo language by Seymour Papert - `http://ccl.northwestern.edu/netlogo`. Get it from `http://ccl.northwestern.edu/netlogo`

    ○ Freemind – A mind mapping application - `http://freemind.sourceforge.net`. Get it from `http://moodle.org/mod/data/view.php?d=13&rid=886`

    ○ Jmol – A chemical structures viewer - `http://jmol.sourceforge.net`. Get it from `http://moodle.org/mod/data/view.php?d=13&rid=88`

- **Game activity module** – Gets input from the quiz and glossary activities in order to play some games such as crosswords, Sudoku, hidden picture, book questions, millionaire, and hangman. Get it from `http://moodle.org/mod/data/view.php?d=13&rid=1196`

Summary

In this final chapter, we looked at copyright issues when using digital works created by others, analyzing some uses that fit under the Fair use umbrella, which is of most interest to teachers and trainers. We also saw other kinds of licenses, such as Creative Commons licenses, that don't just inform us of the allowed uses of the author of a work but also provide a way of licensing our multimedia works on the Web. We also learned how to reference the sources that we use in our creations by using the APA style guide, which is one of many styles available for doing this. Not least, we considered some safety issues when having our students involved in and exposed to larger Web communities, and examined some criteria for selecting Web 2.0 applications to use and communities to be part of. Finally, we looked at some modules and plug-ins that have been developed by Moodle developers, and that can help us develop our Moodle multimedia elements.

After all of these pages, we've finally come to the end of this book. I hope you have found it useful for introducing multimedia in your Moodle courses, and most of all, I hope this new way of doing things brings performance not just for your teaching but particularly for your students' learning. Without this, any effort or innovation is non-sense.

This book was written around a very simple idea—we teachers, trainers, and most of all, students, with free and accessible tools and some basic know-how, can create simple multimedia elements and tasks easily and integrate them in Moodle for learning in our everyday lives. I hope you find this idea useful and more than that, effective. And by using multimedia in Moodle not just as a product for better delivery, but also to improve the ways in which students can construct, you can bring more imagination and learning to your classes.

Index

A

APA (American Psychological Association)
    243
Audacity
  audio, capturing from microphone 100
  audio, remixing 102
  control toolbar 96
  editor toolbar 96
  meter toolbar 96
  mixer toolbar 96
  music tracks, slicing 97
  timeline 96
  tracks 96
  using 95
audio
  activities 90
  CD track, ripping 92-95
  extracting, from CDs using VLC 90-92
  integrating, in Moodle 89
audio, capturing from microphone
  activities 100
  audio input, selecting 100
  audio tracks, importing 102
  capturing, tips 100
  MP3 file size, reducing 102
  sound amplification 102
  tracks, moving in timeline 102
  voice, recording 101
audio, remixing
  Envelope tool used 103
  new track, creating 103
  selections, editing 103
  volume gradients, creating 103
audio formats, free music online
  about 77, 78

  MIDI 78
  MP3 78
  OGG 78
  PCM 77
  WAV 77
  WMA 78

B

basic image formats, free pictures online
  BMP 26
  GIF 26
  JPEG 26
  PNG 26
Bookmarklet tool 121

C

CBR (Constant Bit Rate) 89
comic strips, creating
  elements, adding 65, 66
  elements, editing 66
  features 63
  publishing 66, 67
  Strip Generator, used 64
common multimedia issues, Moodle
  copyright issues 237
  safety issues 244
  Web2.0 application issues 245
copyright issues
  advice seeking, areas 243
  All rights reserved creative work 237
  Creative Commons license, permissions
      241
  Creative Commons license, selecting 242
  Creative Commons license, using 240
  fair use, aspects 238

plagiarism 243
Public domain 239
source, referencing 243
course
  comic strips, creating 63
  content 12
  examples, for developing 22, 23
  free music online, finding 77
  free pictures online, finding 25
  free video online, finding 115
  goal 10
  module themes 12, 13
  Moodle images, inserting 33
  MP3 format usage, reasons 92
  photo capturing, GIMP used 38
  picture enhancement, GIMP used 38
  pre-requisites 13
  screenshots, capturing 60
  slideshows, creating 68
  structure 10, 12
course pre-requisites
  hardware 13-15
  knowledge 13
  software 15
Creative Commons Attribution license 9
custom maps
  creating, Google Maps used 180-187
custom maps, creating
  embedded map, customizing 186
  Google Maps, using 181-87
  lines, adding 185
  linking, to 186
  new map, creating 182
  placemark, adding 182-184
  types, selecting 183

D

digital photo collages, photo capturing
  layers, adding 55, 56
  photo areas, eliminating 56, 57
  text, adding 58, 59
  XCF 55
Dimdim
  meeting, setting up 228-232
  record functionality 235
  using 228

Dipity 177
downloading
  JClic 205
  TeacherTube videos 119, 121
  You Tube videos 119, 121

E

edited movie, Windows Movie Maker
  publishing 134
  edit toolbar, Audacity 96
effects, Windows Movie Maker
  inserting 130
  removing 131
elements, floor plan
  adding 171
elements, GIMP 43
EMBED and OBJECT tags 16
Embed Widget option 180
Envelope tool used, audio 103
Event, interactive timelines
  adding 178, 179
  example, course 22,23

F

Flickr, free pictures online
  about 27
  license 31
  photos, uploading 29, 30
  pictures, saving 29
  pictures, searching 28
floor plan
  creating, floor planner used 167-172
floor plan, creating
  design, saving 171, 172
  draw room icon 170
  elements, adding 171
  embedding, in Moodle 172
  exporting, as image 172
  floor, adding 170
  floor planner, using 167-169
  room, creating 170
floor planner 168
free music online, finding
  Audio Archive 79
  audio formats 77
  CCMixter 80

Freesound 80
Imeem 82, 83
Internet Archive 79
Magnatune site 88
Musopen site 88
Odeo site 88
Soundsnap site 88
free pictures online, finding
about 25
Flickr 27
image formats, basics 26
Shutterstock 32
Stock Exchange 32
Wikimedia Commons 31
free video online, finding
Academic earth 118
Bookmarklet tool 121
Instructables 116
Keepvid option, using 121
Movavi tool 119
Movavi tool, installing 119
output formats 120
Sclipo 117
TeacherTube videos, downloading 119, 121
TrueTube 118
video formats 116
You Tube videos, downloading 119, 121

G

gadgets
creating, Google Doc used 162-167
gadgets, creating
collaborate option 167
Google Doc used 164-167
discuss option 167
inserting 163-165
publishing 166, 167
share option 167
GIMP
about 42
auto white balance function, using 53
brushes element 44
color balance, correcting 52-54
color balance, using 54
downloading 43
elements 43

gradient element 44
image, flipping 52
image, rotating 51, 52
image, selecting 50, 51
image brightness, reducing 54
image contrast, correcting 54
images, cropping 44-47
images, resizing 47-49
images. saving 49-51
image window element 43
layers dialog element 44
levels tools, adjusting 53
main toolbox elements 43
patterns element 44
pictures, editing 42
standard interface, updating 44
tasks 42
tool options element 43
white balance, correcting 52-54
GNU Free Documentation 31
Google Docs
about 162
code, embedding 166
gadgets 162
logging in 163
using 162, 163
Google Maps
advantage 181
embedded map, customizing 186
lines, adding 185
linking to 186
new map, creating 182
placemark, adding 182-184
use 181

H

hardware, course pre-requisites
advanced kit 14
basic requirement 14
low budget kit 14
Hot Potatoes
about 197
advantage 197
excercise, publishing 203
exercises 198
HTML files, integrating with JCross exercise

204
integrating, advantage 205
JCross-crosswords 198-201
JMix-jumble exercises 202, 203
registering 197

I

Imeem, free music online
about 82, 83
audio, uploading 83-85
playlist, creating 85-88
interactive exercises
activity, publishing 216
activity, sequencing 214, 215
creating, JClic used 205, 207
finding pairs activity, creating 213, 214
new project, starting with 207
puzzle activity, creating 208-213
Resource-link, adding to file 216-218
interactive timelines
creating, Dipity used 176-180
interactive timelines, creating
about 176
customising 180
Dipity used 176-180
Embed Widget option 180
event, adding 178, 179
topic, adding 177, 178

J

JClic
about 205
Activities tab 207
downloading 205
interactive activities 205
loading 206
Media library tab 207
Project tab 207
Sequences tab 207
Jing, screenshot capturing
about 62
advantages 62
limitations 63

K

Keepvid option, free video online
using 121

L

layers dialog element, GIMP 44
layers, digital photo collages
adding 55,56
levels tools, GIMP 53
license, Flickr 31
Lightbox gallery activity module 246
lighting, photo capturing 40

M

meeting, real-time classroom
Adobe PDF document, uploading 234
desktop, sharing 233
Microsoft Powerpoint presentation. uploading 234
whiteboard, using 233
mind maps
creating, Mindomo used 173-176
mind maps, creating
Mindomo tool, using 175
Mindomo used 173-176
multimedia elements, adding 174, 175
saving 176
sharing 176
topics, adding 174
YouTube video, adding 175
Mindomo
about 173
Home tab 174
Insert tab 174
using 173-176
Topic and Subtopic option 174
modules and plug-ins list
Application filters 246
Application filters, Freemind 246
Application filters, Geogebra 246
Application filters, Jmol 246
Application filters, Netlogo 246
Dimdim activity module 246
Game activity module 246
Lightbox gallery activity module 246

Skype activity module 246
Stamp activity module 246
Mogulus
  about 148
  using 149
Moodle
  and multimedia, tasks 17
  built-in HTML editor, using 34-38
  common multimedia issues 237-246
  images, inserting 33
  images, uploading as attachments 33, 34
  multimedia 8
Moodle multimedia
  about 9
  benefits 9
  configuring 16, 17
  multimedia artifacts 9
Moodle multimedia, configuring
  EMBED and OBJECT tags, allowing 16
  file size, increasing 16, 17
  HTML editor, using 16
  multimedia plugins, enabling 16
  RSS feeds, enabling 16
multimedia
  adding, to assignments 197
  adding, to lessons 197
  adding, to multiple choice answers 193, 196
  adding, to quizzes 197
  and Moodle, tasks 17
  assessing, rubric tool used 218
  common issues 237, 244-246
  embed code, adding 195
  files, precautions 196
  HREF HTML tag, using 195
  modules and plug-ins list 246
  multiple choice questions, editing 194
  overview 7, 8
multimedia, assessing
  criteria, list 219
  criteria 1 218
  criteria 2 218
  example 218, 219
  use of images criteria 218
Music for an everyday life using Moodle course. *See* **course 9**
music tracks, Audacity
  audio, importing 98

Fade In 99
Fade Out 99
MP3, exporting 99
new audio project, creating 97
slicing 97
track parts, deleting 98
track parts, selecting 98

N

Norwegian Broadcasting (NRK) 13

O

online presentation
  creating, Voicethread used 187-192
online presentation, creating
  about 187
  advantage 187
  comment, adding 190
  comment, sharing 191
  media, uploading 188, 189
  publishing options 191
  uses 187
  Voicethread use 187-192
online TV
  creating, Mogulus used 148-155

P

photo capturing
  basic points 39
  composition 40
  composition, Rule of thirds 40
  digital photo collages, creating 55
  lighting 40
  lighting, aperture 41
  lighting, shutter 40
  size 42
Photo Story, creating
  background music, adding 144
  motion, adding 142, 143
  narration, adding 142, 143
  Photo Story 3 138
  pictures, editing 140
  pictures, importing 139-141
  publishing 144, 145
  starting with 139

titles, adding to pictures 141
pictures
  GIMP, using 42
  learning benefits 38
podcasting
  about 107
  Podomatic used 108-113
pre-requisites, course
  hardware 13-15
  knowledge 13
  software 15

R

real-time classroom, creating
  communication, managing 235
  DimDim tool, using 228
  meeting, recording 235
  meeting, setting up 228-231
  meeting, starting with 233
  online meeting space, connecting to 232
  participation, managing 235
  VoIP tool, disadvantages 228
  web meeting main interface, elements 231, 232
real-time communication
  chat, starting 224
  chat history, disabling 223
  chat settings, configuring 222
  files, transfering 226
  Google Chat 222
  Group chat option, enabling 224-226
  online status, checking 224
  video chat, enabling 226, 227
  video previews, integrating 225
  voice chat, enabling 226, 227
  Voice over IP (VoIP) 222
rubric tool
  example 218
  using 218

S

safety issues
  cyber-bullying, preventing 244
  e-safety, addressing websites 245
  personal details 244
screencast

adding, to Moodle 147
  creating, Jing used 146
  screen recording, with audio 146, 147
screenshots
  capturing, need for 60
  capturing, Jing used 62
  capturing, Print Screen key used 60-62
  capturing, ways 60
Slide, slideshows
  about 73
  add images area 74
  details, entering 75
  editing area 74
Slideshare, slideshows
  about 71
  advantage 71
  presentation, publishing 72
  presentation, uploading 72
slideshows, creating
  about 68
  online photo slideshows, creating 73-75
  Powerpoint slides, exporting as images 68-71
  Slideshare, using 71-73
Soundtrackers 44
stop motion movie, creating
  Animator DV Simple +, using 155-159
Strip Generator
  about 64
  comic strips, publishing 67

T

tasks, Moodle and multimedia
  forum usage, with pictures 18
  forum usage, with sound attachments 19, 20
  forum usage, with videos 21
  images, adding to forums 17, 18
  sound, adding to forums 18
  videos, adding to forums 20-23
text to speech conversion
  voice, assigning to avtar 105, 106
  Voki used 104, 105

U

ukulele instrument 181, 185

V

VBR (Variable Bit Rate) 89
video
  adding, to Moodle 135
  online TV, creating 148, 155
  Photo Story, creating 138
  screencast, creating 146
  stop motion movie, creating 155-159
  uploading, directly to Moodle 135
  uploading, to TeacherTube (YouTube)
      135-137
video, editing
  activities 125
  Windows Movie Maker used 126
video formats, free video online
  about 116
  AVI with XVid or DivX 116
  DV 116
  FLV 116
  MOV 116
  MPEG-2 116
  MPEG-4 116
  WMV 116
videos, creating
  video, editing 125
  video selections, extracting from DVD
      122-125
VLC Media Player
  about 91
  CD track, ripping 92-95
Voice over IP (VoIP)
  using 222
Voicethread
  about 188
  comment, adding 190
  comment, sharing 191
  embedding 192
  media, uploading 188, 189
  picture, adding 188
  publishing options, setting 191, 192
  using 187-192
Voki used, text to speech conversion
      104, 105

W

Web 2.0
  about 161
  gadgets 162
Web2.0 application issues
  backup 245
  community and development team activity
      level 245
  formats 245
  ownership and licensing 245
Wikimedia Commons, free pictures online
      31
Windows Movie Maker, video editing
  about 126
  advantage 127
  collections, creating 128, 129
  edited movie, publishing 134
  effects, inserting 130
  effects, removing 131
  main sections 126
  main video file, importing 129
  movie title at end, inserting 132, 133
  movie title in the beginning, inserting 132
  old sound track, replacing 133
  project, creating 128
  storyboard, creating 130
  transaction, inserting 130, 131
  using 127
  video, splitting 129, 130
WYSIWYG (What You See Is What You Get)
      34

X

XCF, digital photo collages 55

Y

YouTube video
  adding, to mind maps 175
  downloading 119,121

Packt Open Source Project Royalties

When we sell a book written on an Open Source project, we pay a royalty directly to that project. Therefore by purchasing Moodle 1.9 Multimedia, Packt will have given some of the money received to the Moodle project

In the long term, we see ourselves and you—customers and readers of our books—as part of the Open Source ecosystem, providing sustainable revenue for the projects we publish on. Our aim at Packt is to establish publishing royalties as an essential part of the service and support a business model that sustains Open Source.

If you're working with an Open Source project that you would like us to publish on, and subsequently pay royalties to, please get in touch with us.

Writing for Packt

We welcome all inquiries from people who are interested in authoring. Book proposals should be sent to author@packtpub.com. If your book idea is still at an early stage and you would like to discuss it first before writing a formal book proposal, contact us; one of our commissioning editors will get in touch with you.

We're not just looking for published authors; if you have strong technical skills but no writing experience, our experienced editors can help you develop a writing career, or simply get some additional reward for your expertise.

About Packt Publishing

Packt, pronounced 'packed', published its first book "Mastering phpMyAdmin for Effective MySQL Management" in April 2004 and subsequently continued to specialize in publishing highly focused books on specific technologies and solutions.
Our books and publications share the experiences of your fellow IT professionals in adapting and customizing today's systems, applications, and frameworks. Our solution-based books give you the knowledge and power to customize the software and technologies you're using to get the job done. Packt books are more specific and less general than the IT books you have seen in the past. Our unique business model allows us to bring you more focused information, giving you more of what you need to know, and less of what you don't.

Packt is a modern, yet unique publishing company, which focuses on producing quality, cutting-edge books for communities of developers, administrators, and newbies alike. For more information, please visit our website: www.PacktPub.com.

Moodle 1.9 for Teaching
7-14 Year Olds: Beginner's Guide

ISBN:978-1-847197-14-6   Paperback: 236 pages

Effective e-learning for younger students using
Moodle as your Classroom Assistant

1. Focus on the unique needs of young learners
    to create a fun, interesting, interactive, and
    informative learning environment your
    students will want to go on day after day

2. Engage and motivate your students with
    games, quizzes, movies, and podcasts the
    whole class can participate in

3. Go paperless! Put your lessons online and
    grade them anywhere, anytime

Moodle Course Conversion:
Beginner's Guide

ISBN: 978-1-847195-24-1   Paperback: 316 pages

Taking existing classes online quickly with the
Moodle LMS

1. No need to start from scratch! This book shows
    you the quickest way to start using Moodle and
    e-learning, by bringing your existing lesson
    materials into Moodle

2. Move your existing course notes, worksheets,
    and resources into Moodle quickly then
    improve your course, taking advantage of
    multimedia and collaboration

Please check **www.PacktPub.com** for information on our titles

Moodle Administration

ISBN: 978-1-847195-62-3   Paperback: 376 pages

An administrator's guide to configuring, securing, customizing, and extending Moodle

1. A complete guide for planning, installing, optimizing, customizing, and configuring Moodle

2. Secure, back up, and restore your VLE

3. Extending and networking Moodle

4. Detailed walkthroughs and expert advice on best practices

Moodle 1.9 E-Learning Course Development

ISBN: 978-1-847193-53-7   Paperback: 384 pages

A complete guide to successful learning using Moodle

1. Updated for Moodle version 1.9

2. Straightforward coverage of installing and using the Moodle system

3. A unique course-based approach focuses your attention on designing well-structured, interactive, and successful courses

Please check **www.PacktPub.com** for information on our titles